LOVE IS A CHOICE WORKBOOK

Dr. Robert Hemfelt

Dr. Frank Minirth

Dr. Paul Meier

Dr. Deborah and Dr. Brian Newman

A
JANET
THOMA
BOOK

THOMAS NELSON PUBLISHERS
Nashville

THE MINIRTH-MEIER CLINIC OFFICES

National Headquarters
MINIRTH-MEIER, CLINIC, P.A.
2100 N. Collins Blvd.
Richardson, Texas 75080
(214) 669-1733
1-800-229-3000
OUTPATIENT SERVICES
DAY TREATMENT CENTER
HOSPITAL PROGRAMS

MINIRTH-MEIER TUNNELL &
WILSON CLINIC
Centre Creek Office Plaza, Suite 200
1812 Centre Creek Drive
Austin, Texas 78754
(512) 339-7511
1-800-444-5751
OUTPATIENT SERVICES
DAY TREATMENT CENTER
HOSPITAL PROGRAMS

MINIRTH-MEIER CLINIC
WEST
260 Newport Center Drive, Suite 430
Newport Beach, California 92660
(714) 760-3112
1-800-877-4673
OUTPATIENT SERVICES
DAY TREATMENT CENTER
HOSPITAL PROGRAMS

MINIRTH-MEIER CLINIC, P.C.
The Grove, Suite 1510
2100 Manchester Road
Wheaton, Illinois 60187
(708) 653-1717
1-800-848-8872
1-800-545-1819
OUTPATIENT SERVICES
DAY TREATMENT CENTER
HOSPITAL PROGRAMS
NATIONAL COMMUNICATIONS
DIVISION

MINIRTH-MEIER-RICE
CLINIC, P.A.
Koger Center in the Shannon Building
10801 Executive Center Drive, Suite 305
Little Rock, Arkansas 72211
(501) 225-0576
1-800-488-4769
OUTPATIENT SERVICES
HOSPITAL PROGRAMS

MINIRTH-MEIER BYRD
CLINIC, P.A.
4300 Fair Lakes Court, Suite 200
Fairfax, Virginia 22033-4231
(703) 968-3556
1-800-486-HOPE (4673)
OUTPATIENT SERVICES
DAY TREATMENT CENTER
HOSPITAL PROGRAMS

For general information about other Minirth-Meier Clinic branch offices, counseling services, educational resources and hospital programs, call toll-free 1-800-545-1819.

National Headquarters: (214) 669-1733   1-800-229-3000

Published in Nashville, Tennessee, by Thomas Nelson, Inc., and distributed in Canada by Lawson Falle, Ltd., Cambridge, Ontario.

Scripture quotations are from the NEW KING JAMES VERSION of the Bible. Copyright © 1979, 1980, 1982, Thomas Nelson, Inc., Publishers.

Printed in the United States of America
3 4 5 6 7 — 96 95 94 93

CONTENTS

PART THREE
Defining Healthy Relationships

Acknowledgments

The authors wish to thank the many people who helped to make the publication of *Love Is a Choice Workbook* a reality. We especially want to acknowledge the friendship, vision, direction, and editing of Janet Thoma. We also thank Lois Keefer for her editorial assistance in bringing the manuscript to life, as well as her personal contribution to this project. Thanks to the wonderful staff at Thomas Nelson Publishers, especially Bruce Barbour and Bob Zaloba for their friendship and support during the project. We also thank Carol Mandt of the Minirth-Meier Clinics. Without her this project would have been much more difficult. Most of all, we want to thank our families for their encouragement and patience during the completion of this workbook.

PART ONE

THE CAUSES OF CODEPENDENCY

1. GETTING STARTED

Jennifer Fortisi was frantic as she entered the counseling session. "I read that book on codependency you asked me to, and I think everyone must be codependent. You doctors have really gone too far this time. You have discovered a disease that everyone has."

"Does that mean that you found yourself identifying with codependency, Jennifer?" Dr. Hemfelt patiently responded.

"That's not the issue here, the issue is whether everyone suffers from codependency."

"Jennifer, I have to tell you that the sad reality is that codependency is an epidemic issue. But that isn't a reason to be fatalistic about it and decide that there is nothing we can do to change. On the contrary, there is a lot you can do to make your relationships better. Relationships are essential to every aspect of our lives. Did you find yourself in the book you read?" Dr. Hemfelt asked once again.

"Yes, I suppose I did. I just don't know what to do about it. All I know is that Al wants to leave me, and my life is falling apart. If what I have is codependency and what I need is love, I'm open to your suggestions. I just can't imagine life without him."

"Are you willing to look at yourself?" asked Dr. Hemfelt.

"Yes, as long as it will bring Al back," Jennifer stated emphatically.

"Jennifer, I don't have any more control over Al than you do. I cannot guarantee that your changing and looking at yourself will bring him back, but I can tell you that if you work on yourself some change will occur. It will be meaningful change whether it makes your marriage last or not."

That's how Jennifer began her journey to recovery. This workbook is an avenue to help you focus on situations in your life that have led to your codependent behavior and to work toward healing yourself. Our goal is to help you establish healthy relationships based on genuine love.

Are You Codependent?

Some people, like Jennifer, have no idea what issues or thoughts make them so desperate. Others have identified their pain, but need to learn how to get through it. Though readers may share common unhealthy behaviors and feelings of hopelessness, each person has been through a set of unique experiences that have led to these problems. You are a human being, created in God's image. Be careful of labeling yourself as a codependent in an unhealthy way. Instead, use the label to face the unhealthy behaviors going on in your life. Don't use it to shame yourself.

Let's begin by identifying where you are in your codependent behavior. Check the statements from the following list that fit your life.

1. _____ I can't stand to be alone.
2. _____ I am a perfectionist.
3. _____ I am driven by the approval of others.
4. _____ I feel desperate when I cannot gain the approval of other people.
5. _____ I find myself making decisions based on how they will affect other people and rarely consider myself.
6. _____ Many times I feel obsessed by a need for total order in my life.

7. ____ I put work first, above anything.

8. ____ I find myself adjusting to my spouse's needs rather than communicating my feelings.

9. ____ I do not experience anger.

10. ____ I overeat often.

11. ____ I am constantly wondering what other people think of me.

12. ____ I cover up my feelings so others won't realize what I really think.

13. ____ I am afraid that if others really knew me they would run and hide.

14. ____ I am constantly trying to figure how to stay ahead in my relationships.

15. ____ I cover up my feelings of self-doubt with drug or alcohol use.

16. ____ I can't say no when I am asked to do a favor or serve on a committee.

17. ____ When I begin to feel sad or angry I go shopping, work harder, or eat.

18. ____ I tell myself it shouldn't hurt so much when others let me down.

19. ____ I need to control those close to me.

20. ____ I need everyone to be happy with me so that I can feel good about myself.

21. ____ I need others to be strong for me without requiring anything from me in return.

If you checked two or more of the preceding statements, you have some codependent issues that are worth looking at.

Jennifer raised a good question when she wondered if everyone in the world is codependent. She was obviously suspicious that the doctors were conspiring to find some disease for which everyone would need treatment. If you have done some reading about codependence, you've probably already recognized unhealthy patterns of behavior in yourself, your parents, your children, or even your friends.

Dr. Frank Minirth says, "All families are somewhat codependent or dysfunctional. That's natural, since none of us is perfect. All of our parents have made some mistakes and passed some of their pain on to us, and we'll pass some of that pain on to our own children." This isn't a reason to put down this workbook. Look over the issues you identified in the list above. These represent areas where codependency is robbing you of joy in life. Do you want to change those desperately unhappy feelings? You can, by making a commitment to work openly and honestly through these pages.

How to Use This Workbook

Begin with the first lesson and work right through to the end. All the lessons are important, and each one builds on the others. As you go through the book, you'll encounter a variety of exercises with helpful examples to get you started. If you don't understand a particular exercise, don't let yourself feel stupid or different. A workbook is not able to give you the kind of helpful feedback a counselor would. This is why many people choose to do the book in the context of counseling or a support group. It will be important for you to have someone you can call to discuss some of your questions, thoughts, and feelings, whether it be a counselor, a support group, or a friend.

Many of the exercises will involve writing letters or telling about your feelings and experiences. It is important for you to open yourself up as you write. Allow your feelings to flow freely without judgment or evaluation. Forget about proper grammar. Don't edit or rewrite. No English teacher is going to check your work with a red pen! If you can't think of what to write, try free association. Ask yourself questions, and then answer them. For example, think about why it's hard for you to do the exercise—"Why don't I like to think about my family?"—until you open up to the answer.

Find a safe place to keep your book. It is important for you to feel that your thoughts and feelings will remain private. You may want to share some of this material with other people, but you should be able to determine when and how much.

The chapters in this workbook follow the sequence of chapters in *Love Is a Choice*. We recommend that you read the book while you do the workbook. Give yourself time to do every chapter carefully and thoughtfully so you can gain something from each exercise. Don't rush through the book—it's not a good idea to do more than three lessons a week. Four or six months to a year is a good pace to set for yourself. Please understand that it isn't just getting through the book that promotes healing. Healing comes as you carefully and consistently apply what you learn to your life.

Make a commitment to work regularly in this book, just as if you were keeping a business appointment. Choose a time when you can work at a leisurely pace without being interrupted. Mark it down on your calendar.

When will you schedule time to work in this book? *(For instance, Tuesday mornings from 9:00–9:45.)*

Day of the week: _____

Time of day: _____

The setting is also important. Choose a place that is comfortable, where there are no distractions, and where you can be free to express your emotions.

Where will you work on your workbook? _____

Support Network

This workbook is not a substitute for counseling. At the Minirth-Meier Clinics we often use workbooks in group and individual counseling to guide a person through the recovery process. You may need other people to act as sounding boards or encouragers as you work through the material presented here. You can fill this need with a network of emotionally healthy friends, by joining a support group, or by seeking professional counseling. At the end of this chapter you will find a list of support groups.

List the names of groups and individuals who might be part of your support network.

<table>
<tr><td>Friends</td><td>Support Groups</td></tr>
<tr><td>_____</td><td>_____</td></tr>
<tr><td>_____</td><td>_____</td></tr>
<tr><td>_____</td><td>_____</td></tr>
<tr><td>_____</td><td>_____</td></tr>
<tr><td>_____</td><td>_____</td></tr>
<tr><td>_____</td><td>_____</td></tr>
<tr><td>_____</td><td>_____</td></tr>
</table>

As you work through this book, you will experience moments of deep joy as you recognize and release yourself from negative patterns in your life. You'll also encounter anger and grief as you confront painful truths about your past and present relationships. All of these experiences will lead to a fuller understanding of what true love is and how you've been missing out on it. We can't guarantee that you can change the lives of the ones you love, but you can change your own life and the way you relate to other people, which will make your recovery very worthwhile.

Begin now by taking some time to think about and describe what you're feeling about starting this workbook experience. Express your thoughts in a letter to yourself. Think of it as the dedication of a book. Write about what you hope to gain from this experience.

To get you started, we have included Jennifer's letter as an example.

Dear Jennifer,

      You're exhausted, depressed, and desperate. You don't know what you should do. You're not absolutely certain Dr. Hemfelt can help you, but where else can you go? Al and the girls mean the world to you. You've got to try hard to understand what's gone wrong and what you can do to make it better. Hang in there, Jennifer—give it your best!

Dear _____,

_____

_____

_____

_____

_____

_____

_____

_____

_____

_____

_____

      We would like to end this chapter by telling you that you are special. Psalm 139:14 says that you are fearfully and wonderfully made. You are unique. You have dignity and worth. Someday you will read those words and believe them. You will no longer need to use your codependent behavior to make you feel alive and worthwhile. We hope this workbook helps you sift through the webs of your present relationships to find the healing God has for you.

This workbook is for you. We hope that it enriches your life as you journey toward recovery from codependency.

THOUGHT CHECK

One thing that I've done that I can feel good about is _____

_____

_____

I need to follow up on _____

_____

_____

An important new insight I've gained is that _____

_____

_____

_____

2. WHAT IS CODEPENDENCY?

Codependency is living the myth that you can make yourself happy by trying to control people and events outside yourself. A sense of control, or the lack of it, is central to everything you do and think.

Jennifer Fortisi is the ultimate supermom. She's the president of the PTA, Brownie leader, and teacher's aide. At church she leads a Bible study and coordinates meals for shut-ins. Her house is spotless, she volunteers at the library and runs a veritable taxi service from her shining-clean station wagon, shuttling kids to and from ballet, karate, church, clubs, and school activities.

Why would anyone create such a hopelessly overwhelming schedule? Jennifer's father was an alcoholic. She never knew what love and security felt like. Her parents never attended a single school function. Their house was always full of trash and filth. And now Jennifer is trying to fix all those things in her past by being the perfect wife and mother. All her frantic activity leaves her exhausted and depressed, with little emotional energy left for the kind of nurturance and love her children really need. Unless Jennifer deals with her compulsive need to control everything about her family's life, her children will grow up with the same sense of abandonment and neglect that marred her own childhood.

Codependency is an epidemic. Roughly one hundred million Americans across two concurrent generations suffer problems of codependency. You are not exempt from the problem. The despair codependency has caused in your life is the reason you decided to pick up this workbook.

Let's begin by describing the traits of codependents and identifying which of them are found in your life.

I. The Codependent Is Driven by One or More Compulsions

Compulsions are easy to identify if they are considered "bad," like addiction to drugs, alcohol, sex, physical abuse of others, or eating disorders. Work-related compulsions are much more subtle. Our society admires people who keep an immaculate house, get the top sales dollar, or make straight A's. But the people who display these admirable qualities are often the unhappy victims of their own compulsive behavior.

> What are the compulsions in your life? *(For instance, do you have to check the stove and lights several times before you leave the house? Are you always thinking about food, sex, money, or fitness?)*

1. _____

2. _____

3. _____

4. _____

5. _____

II. The Codependent Is Bound and Tormented by the Way Things Were in the Dysfunctional Family of Origin

No one grows up in a home where all needs are met all the time. In cases where the family is severely dysfunctional—like Jennifer's—the pain is likely to pass from generation to generation. Jennifer's father was a compulsive drinker. Jennifer became a compulsive volunteer.

In the previous question you identified your own compulsions. Now think back to your family of origin (the family in which you were raised as a child). What compulsive behaviors do you remember among those family members?

Did your parents have the same compulsions you do?

_____ yes _____ no

How did they model this type of behavior for you? *(For instance, my mother always made us take off our shoes so we wouldn't track dirt in the house; my father flew into a rage if we got poor grades.)*

1. _____

2. _____

3. _____

4. _____

5. _____

Many times we develop our compulsions in reaction to our unmet emotional needs. What are some unmet, or partially unmet, emotional needs that you have?

1. _____ I'm afraid of being abandoned.
2. _____ I don't feel as if anyone will stand up for me or protect me.
3. _____ Nobody cares how I'm feeling.
4. _____ The finances are all in my lap, and I'm frightened.
5. _____ No one's willing to listen to me when I have problems.
6. _____ I can't remember the last time I was on the receiving end of a gesture of love and affection.

7. _____ My family is very standoffish; we don't hug each other.
8. _____ People expect my help but never express their appreciation.
9. _____ No one reaches out to me when I'm feeling down.
10. _____ I sometimes wonder if there'll be a roof over my head next week.
11. _____ I work hard and do well, but no one cares.

12. _____ _____

13. _____ _____

14. _____ _____

III. The Codependent's Self-Esteem Is Very Low

"You're very important to me, do you know that?"
"You did a great job—I'm really proud of you."
"Thanks a lot, sweetheart, I really appreciate your help."
Children from dysfunctional families may grow to adulthood without hearing any of these very important messages about value, worth, and dignity. They end up feeling empty and worthless, like they're missing something that everyone else has. Codependents look desperately to others for their self-esteem, unconsciously thinking, *If only I can get other people to approve of me, then maybe I'll start feeling good about myself.*

These questions are designed to help you confront some self-esteem issues in your life.

Do you defend yourself from unfair criticism?   _____ yes _____ no

Do you criticize yourself before others have a chance to?
_____ yes _____ no

Do others consider you overconfident, while deep inside you feel just the opposite?   _____ yes _____ no

Would you want someone like yourself as a best friend?

_____ yes _____ no

Are you constantly nagging yourself with self-critical thoughts?

_____ yes _____ no

What are some of the common critical comments you make about yourself? *(For instance, that was a stupid thing to do; I know those people won't like me; I never get anything right.)*

_____

_____

_____

_____

_____

On a scale of one to ten (ten being high self-esteem) what number would you assign to your self-esteem? _____

IV. The Codependent Is Certain His or Her Happiness Hinges on Others

Codependents have an unconscious drive to fix the unhappy things in their past by manipulating people and events. Jennifer felt abandoned and unloved as a child. Now her happiness is tied to whether or not she can make her children think they have the perfect mother. Emotionally healthy people recognize that they can't control other people and events.

Let's say that Sam drives into a busy gas station, pumps gas into his car, and then cleans the windshield. A furious attendant comes out and yells at him to move on because other people are waiting. If Sam's self-esteem is low, he will think, *He's right—I'm stupid and selfish, and everyone can see it. I deserve to be yelled at.* Fifteen minutes later, Ralph pulls into the same gas station, pumps gas, cleans his windshield, and gets the same furious reaction from the attendant. Ralph's emotionally healthy response is *Boy, is that guy being unreasonable! He must be having a bad day.*

Ralph realized he couldn't control the attendant's attitude, so he let the comment slide off. Sam felt overpowered by the attendant's unreasonable criticism, and let his self-esteem sink a little lower.

Do you accept criticism without stopping to consider whether the other person is being reasonable and fair? ____ yes ____ no

Do you find yourself thinking, *If certain people would treat me better, then I could be happy?* ____ yes ____ no

Do you react to harsh treatment by thinking, *I deserve it?* ____ yes ____ no

V. The Codependent Feels Inordinately Responsible for Others

Many codependents try to avoid their own pain by taking on other people's problems. If a best friend's marriage breaks up, the codependent thinks, *I should have been able to help them solve their problems.* Codependents can't manage their own lives successfully—much less everyone else's—so they end up feeling guilty about everything.

Do you have a deep sense of responsibility and/or guilt for the decisions and feelings of other people in your life? ____ yes ____ no

What people? *(For instance, children, friends, boss.)*

1. _____

2. _____

3. _____

What issues? *(For instance, did I give them enough help with their homework—will they make it in school? Will my friend be okay at work after we've had a fight?)*

1. _____

2. _____

3. _____

Do you think it's your fault when your friends or family are hurting? _____ yes _____ no

Do you think you could do something to stop their pain even when it doesn't concern you? _____ yes _____ no

Describe how you have tried by writing the names of significant people that you take responsibility for.

1. _____

2. _____

3. _____

How do you feel you could stop their pain?

1. _____

2. _____

3. _____

VI. The Codependent's Relationship with a Spouse or Significant Other Person is Marred by a Damaging, Unstable Lack of Balance Between Dependence and Independence

God created us to be both dependent and independent. In the end we are ultimately responsible for our own welfare—no other person can be expected to care for all of our needs. On the other hand, God created within us the need for companionship, both with Him and with significant others. Co-dependents constantly find themselves at extremes in their relationships. It's either, "I can't live without you" or "I can make it on my own without you or anyone else."

Do you find yourself feeling like a yo-yo on a string, bouncing back and forth between independence and dependence with significant others? _____ yes _____ no

How? *(For instance, I asked my parents to help on our mortgage, then I got angry and wouldn't speak to them for three months.)*

_____

_____

_____

I recognize these very dependent behaviors in myself:
(For instance, I can never solve a problem without talking to several people about it; I'm always borrowing money from parents or friends.)

_____

_____

_____

I recognize these very independent behaviors in myself:
(For instance, I keep my feelings to myself; I won't ever ask for help.)

_____

_____

_____

VII. The Codependent Is a Master of Denial and Repression

Counselors never cease to be amazed at how effectively denial works. One of the first questions put to patients at the Minirth-Meier Clinics is "Tell me about your childhood." They invariably respond with something like, "I grew up in a pretty good home," then go on to tell about terribly abusive situations. The denial that helped them survive childhood almost always stands in the way of healing as an adult.

How would you describe your parents?

Mom: _____

_____

_____

Dad: _____

_____

_____

Is it hard for you to admit negative things about your parents?
_____ yes _____ no

Were there any statements such as, "He really wasn't that bad" or "She did the best she could"?   _____ yes _____ no

Did you describe both the good and the bad impact they had on you?   _____ yes _____ no

Did you feel the need to make excuses for your parents' behavior?
_____ yes _____ no

What kind? *(For instance, no one is perfect; they did the best they could.)*

_____

_____

_____

If it's difficult for you to see some faults in your parents, you may be denying some of the problems that lie at the very root of your codependency.

VIII. The Codependent Worries about Things He or She Can't Change and May Well Keep on Trying to Change Them

Codependents cling to a strong set of *if only's. If only I could have managed the children better my husband wouldn't have blown up like that. If only I could make Erica love me, she wouldn't run around with other men.* Codependents just don't buy the truth that we can't control other people.

Can you think of three people in your world you most want to change? *(For instance, husband, mother.)*

1. _____

2. _____

3. _____

How have you tried to change each of these people? *(For instance, I've tried to get him to stop drinking; I've tried to stop her from being so critical.)*

1. _____

2. _____

3. _____

Have your efforts to change these people been effective?

1. _____ yes _____ no

2. _____ yes _____ no

3. _____ yes _____ no

IX. The Codependent's Life Is Punctuated by Extremes

Tom Brinkman is a highly respected deacon at his church, where he's known as a deeply spiritual man and a wise leader. At work Tom has to answer to three different superiors, so he's constantly in a subservient position. He's quiet, efficient, and well-liked. At home Tom is a rageaholic who terrorizes his family with verbal abuse. One misplaced toy is enough to set him off. If Tom's church friends were to see a videotape of his behavior at home, they would never believe it.

If people at work, your friends, and your family were to describe you, would you sound like the same person? _____ yes _____ no

How would they describe you? *(For instance, would your spouse describe you as hard to get along with or easy-going? Would the people at work agree?)*

Home: _____

_____

Work: _____

_____

Church/social setting: _____

_____

Write about the extremes you see in yourself. *(For instance, do you hoard and then spend? Rage and then act tender and loving?)*

Sometimes I _____,

then go to the other extreme by _____

_____

Sometimes I _____,

then go to the other extreme by _____

_____

Sometimes I _____,

then go to the other extreme by _____

_____

X. The Codependent Is Continually Looking for the Something That Is Missing in Life

Codependents struggle through life like a car running on fumes, sputtering its way to the gas station. The messages of worth and dignity they missed in their childhood have left a big empty space. In despair they look outside themselves to find meaning and purpose in life.

Do you feel restless or discontent regardless of your circumstances? _____ yes _____ no

What symptoms of restlessness and discontent do you see in yourself? *(For instance, I wish I could be married. If I could get that promotion I'd be happy. Why don't people notice me and include me in their conversations?)*

1. _____

2. _____

3. _____

Is Time the Great Healer?

Codependency will not improve with time. It will not get better tomorrow. It will get worse. There are steps you can take to help you reverse your descent into misery, but you must take them. They won't just happen. Much depends on your desire to free yourself from the ghosts of your past—the causes of codependency, which we'll discuss in future chapters.

Copy this statement in your own handwriting on the lines below.

I am acting in codependent ways. Time won't stop the misery and desperation. But there is hope. I can change my behavior with God's help.

_____

_____

_____

_____

Congratulations! You have begun an important step to recovery from codependency. You have found the courage to look at yourself. Perhaps in doing this chapter you wrote down some things that were difficult for you to admit. That's good. Healing doesn't come by ignoring your pain and thinking it will go away. You must accept it, face it, and decide how you're going to change.

Right now you are in a time of self-realization, recognizing the issues you need to deal with. There will be time to change in the future. But first you must open yourself up even more.

3. RUNNING ON EMPTY

We each have within us a God-given hunger for love. The counselors at Minirth-Meier Clinics refer to this hunger as a "love tank." Imagine a heart-shaped reservoir deep inside you. When you were a tiny baby, this love tank was empty. If your parents were both emotionally healthy people with full love tanks of their own, they spent a few decades filling your love tank from theirs. This is the way God designed it to be.

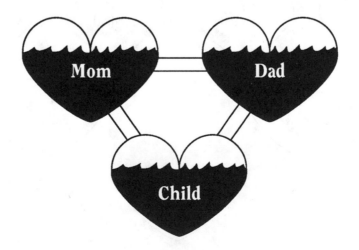

But suppose one of your parents was "running on empty," with a love tank so low that there was little or nothing left to give to you. If that was the case, then it is very likely that you are still carrying the scars of a love-deprived childhood.

Louise came into the clinic with her marriage in shreds. Her husband, Rob, was on the verge of leaving her to escape her compulsive, controlling behavior. Rob wasn't allowed to make any decisions or financial commitments without first consulting her—Louise insisted on having the final say in everything. And she was obsessed by jealousy, always demanding to know what went on at work between Rob and his secretaries. Louise's problems began with an empty childhood love tank. Her father had multiple affairs. His preoccupation with sex left him emotionally absent from the home. Little Louise got no nurturance at all from her father. Louise's mother met all her physical needs, but emotionally she was so involved in trying to hang on to a wayward husband that she had little left in her love tank to pass on to her daughter. The pain and emptiness Louise carried with her from childhood nearly destroyed her marriage.

Now let's focus on the flow of love in your family and how it has affected you. This chart shows three generations, from your grandparents to

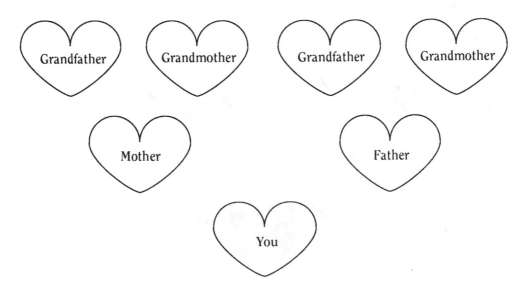

you. Think about these people individually and try to estimate how much love you think was in their love tanks. Fill in the hearts to show the appropriate level. If you have stepparents, add them to the parent's side. How does your love tank look coming out of childhood?

Now draw a new diagram, beginning with yourself. You can't change the love flow of previous generations, but you can change the way things are now. God offers to replace your pain and emptiness with His love expressed directly through His Spirit and indirectly through the new healthy support relationships He may open for your life. He will do everything for you that your parents never did—give you nurturance, guidance, protection, and love. When God heals your pain and fills your love tank, then you'll be able to give to others the love they need from you.

Draw your love tank as full as you would like it to be. Add hearts for the significant people in your life. If you're single, include the people who make up your support group. If you're married, include your spouse and children. Make this diagram show how you hope the future will look. Remember, the presence of God in your life makes your dream a possibility.

Working through these exercises may have stirred up some anger or resentment in you. Write what you are feeling in a letter to yourself. Describe the reality of your love tank right now. Describe your feelings of emptiness and hurt about how little love and nurturance you received when you were growing up. It's important to acknowledge in your letter that your need for love was (and is) legitimate. Sometimes people who feel an overwhelming need for love they've never received begin to think they're crazy for wanting it in the first place. Wrong! You must have a full love tank to lead an emotionally healthy life. End your letter by acknowledging God's love for you.

Dear ————————————,

_____

_____

_____

_____

_____

_____

_____

_____

_____

If you don't receive love, will your love tank stay empty? No. Just as air fills every empty space, so also something fills up that tank.

The heart on page 29 represents your heart as a child. What filled your empty love tank in the place of appropriate parental nurturing? *(For instance, an overemphasis on sex, sports, good grades, friends.)*

Money is almost always a central issue with people whose love tanks are running low. How we handle money is a strong reflection of how we feel about ourselves and how we deal with relationships. Financial affairs are a

very sensitive barometer of codependency because money has a lot to do with two basic elements of our existence: discipline and nurturance.

Check the statements in each of the following categories that describe you. Record the total number of checks you make in each category.

CATEGORY A

1. _____ I keep as much money in the bank as I can and spend little on myself and others.
2. _____ After the house payments, bills, etc., I put most of my money in the bank or into investments.
3. _____ I must control the finances to keep my spouse from spending all the money.
4. _____ I rarely splurge on myself or others.
5. _____ When I spend money, it's usually on a wise investment such as a house or a painting.

Total _____

If you checked several items in Category A, you are a *hoarder*. You are probably very rigid with yourself. You don't let people get to know you very well. You're afraid of being used by others. Your love tank is empty, and you try to fill it with financial security. You keep to yourself for fear of being rejected or used.

CATEGORY B

1. ____ I spend more money on myself than on others.
2. ____ After the bills are paid, my favorite thing to do is buy myself something new.
3. ____ At times I spend more than I have on myself, and I feel guilty.
4. ____ I feel best when I'm shopping for myself.
5. ____ The first person I think of when I'm shopping is myself.
6. ____ Even when I'm shopping for others, I usually come home with something for me.

Total ____

If you found yourself identifying with the statements in Category B, you may be a *self-centered spender*. You probably have an empty love tank, which you try to fill up with possessions. You think that having things will make you feel better about yourself. You have a tendency to relate to people you can use to make you feel better about yourself. You need attention and appreciation from others. You have little love to give to yourself, and the love you give to others is usually intended to buy their love.

CATEGORY C

1. ____ I am always thinking of ways to spend money on others.
2. ____ I buy myself basic needs, but rarely indulge myself with something special.
3. ____ I always see things I wish I could buy for others.
4. ____ Many times I spend more than I have on others.

5. _____ When I shop for myself I usually come home with something for someone else.

6. _____ I don't like to shop for myself.

Total _____

Did you recognize yourself in this section? Then you may be an *others-centered spender*. Because of your empty love tank, you think little of yourself. You feel that your wants or desires are of little value compared to the needs of others. You were probably denied love as a child and have come to believe that love is not available to you. You don't try to get love by your purchases. When you are thanked, you belittle your efforts. You think so little of yourself that you don't even think you deserve praise.

CATEGORY D

1. _____ I just love to spend money, whether on myself or on others.

2. _____ I am always up to the limit on my credit cards and spend more money than I earn.

3. _____ When I feel sad or depressed I go shopping.

4. _____ Shopping makes me feel good and forget about the bad things in my life.

5. _____ I can't pass up a bargain, even though I don't really need the thing I'm purchasing.

6. _____ I live in constant financial instability because of my spending habits.

Total _____

If you checked several items in this category, you may be a *compulsive spender*. You use excitement to fill your empty love tank. You use money to get a natural high by taking risks. Your love tank is so empty that it doesn't matter if you lose, since you don't believe you have much to lose. But if you win, you believe you will win everything.

CATEGORY E

1. ____ I like to show people the things I buy.
2. ____ The real thrill of having something new is the reaction I get from others.
3. ____ I feel a person's worth is measured by the amount of money he or she has.
4. ____ I like knowing that I have nicer things than most of my friends and family.
5. ____ I always pick up the tab at dinner; it makes me feel important.
6. ____ I feel good or bad about myself, depending on how I think others view my financial standing.

Total ____

If this set of statements reflects your attitude about money, you are a *prestige spender*. You have come to believe that your worth is equal to your bank account and your possessions. You may spend on others so that they will come to realize that you are significant and important. You have tried to fill your empty love tank with belongings and possessions. They feel meaningful for a time, but when the newness wears off you need more and more.

Look back over this survey and note the two categories in which you had the most checks. These are the areas you need to work on.

Now let's go back to the love tank idea. Remember that an empty love tank will fill up with something else. What have you learned today about the status of your love tank? In the heart on page 33, write the things, events, and people who fill your love tank today. You may write some of the same things that appeared in your childhood heart, but some may be new.

What counterfeit means are you pursuing to make you feel loved? (*For instance, possessive relationships—give names—alcohol, drugs, work, money, spending, prestige, possessions.*)

Below is a picture of your heart the way it can look after your recovery. Write your name on the top of the heart as you visualize your hopes for recovery. What *new* authentic sources of love and fellowship do you envision for your recovery love tank? *(For instance, an enhanced marriage, the support of a recovery group, a trusting bond with a therapist, renewed spirituality.)*

Four-Layer Cake

Dr. Hemfelt likes to use the illustration of a four-layer cake to show patients how their codependency works. Most people think they can handle their problems by dealing with the symptoms. The four-layer cake shows how important it is to dig deeper into your past experiences, right down to the hurtful things in your childhood that caused your codependency in the first place.

The top layer of the cake consists of symptoms you can see. In Louise's case, the visible symptom of codependency was her overpowering need for control in her marriage. Other "top-layer" symptoms could be addictions, including the non-substance abuses, such as workaholism, rageaholism, and behavioral compulsions. The next layer down (the second layer) is the relationship level. Codependents give themselves distorted internal messages about their relationships with others. Louise's relationship distortion was her belief that she had to control everything in her husband's life in order to get love from him. The third layer is some form of abuse. Louise identified her abuse as being abandoned by her father when she was thirteen. The fourth layer is the hunger for love that is as much a part of us as is breathing. Louise's love hunger resulted from an emotionally distant father and a mother who was preoccupied with the pain and fear of abandonment caused by the father's multiple affairs.

If you look at the cake from the bottom up, you will find that the layer beneath has caused or set up the surface layers. To stop the addictions, compulsions, and visible symptoms, you need to identify the contributing factors from the lower layers. Let's construct your four-layer cake now, beginning at the top and working down.

Layer 1: Identify one or more symptoms of codependency that are visible in your life right now. *(For instance, rageaholism, the need to control others, excessive shyness, being a people pleaser.)*

_____

_____

Why do you behave this way? *(For instance, I'm afraid of being hurt; I'm sure other people won't like me.)*

_____

_____

Layer 2: Think about your close relationships. What are the repeated patterns in all your major relationships? *(For instance, I feel that I am always trying to prove my worth to others and I repeatedly feel abandoned by others.)*

_____

_____

Layer 3: What kind of abuse did you experience in your childhood? *(For instance, my mother screamed at me all the time; I was terrified by my father's behavior when he was drunk.)*

_____

_____

Can you see how this abuse relates to the symptoms you wrote down in Layer 1? *(For instance, during my childhood my mother always criticized me, and now I try like crazy to please everyone.)*

During my childhood _____

_____

and now I _____

_____

Layer 4: Rate the residual love hunger from your childhood experiences on a scale of one to ten, one being a very empty love tank and ten being a full love tank.

I would rate my childhood love tank at (circle one)

1   2   3   4   5   6   7   8   9   10

Are you beginning to see how your current symptoms of codependency have roots in your childhood? _____ yes _____ no

Louise's four-layer cake looks something like this.

Layer 1: Symptoms

Layer 2: Relationship
          distortions

Layer 3: Abuse

Layer 4: Love hunger

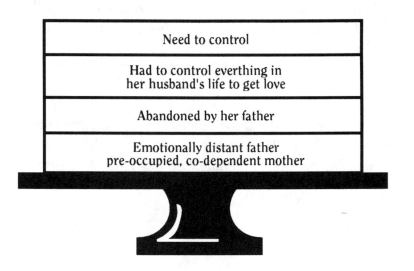

Now fill in your own four-layer cake with the information you gave in response to the questions on page 37.

Layer 1: Symptoms

Layer 2: Relationship
          distortions

Layer 3: Abuse

Layer 4: Love hunger

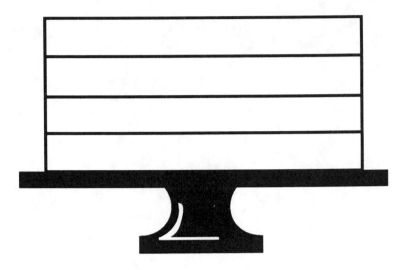

If you've worked through these exercises carefully, you've come a long way toward understanding how your unconscious needs and events for the past affect your present behavior. In the next few chapters we'll ask you to do a little more digging.

THOUGHT CHECK

One thing that I've done that I can feel good about is _____

_____

_____

I need to follow up on _____

_____

_____

An important new insight I've gained is that _____

_____

4. THE WELL-HIDDEN TRUTH

As Roger worked through these chapters he began to recall the emptiness he had felt as a boy. This successful, well-dressed businessman literally wailed and wept as he recounted feelings of being utterly overwhelmed when his father left him in charge of the migrant workers who came to harvest their crops. At age ten he was left to supervise men twice his age who could hardly speak English. And if the tasks weren't finished in the amount of time his father stipulated, Roger was held accountable.

Roger hated meeting his father in the barn after work. His father would consistently become outraged and chase him around, beating him with a belt and screaming at him for not obeying orders. "I just wasn't good enough," Roger cried. "That's why I got beaten—I deserved those bruises!"

It's amazing to sit in counseling sessions and listen to patients recount similar incidents of abuse without even beginning to realize that the treatment they received was truly abusive. Roger believed that what his father had done was right. If the crew of migrant workers wasn't able to complete the required task, Roger thought his father was justified in following through on religious injunctions that caution parents about sparing the rod and spoiling the child.

This inability to recognize blatantly abusive treatment is called *denial*.

Roger never realized the impact of those times with his father until he attended a counseling session thirty years later. He had denied his utter fear of his father and his feelings of total inadequacy that began during those childhood confrontations in the barn. What's even more amazing is that Roger completely denied that abuse had ever occurred.

We have a deep need for our love tanks to be filled. We also have a deep need to hide from the fact that they haven't been filled. That's where denial comes into the picture, and that's also why it's so hard to recognize. Once we break down the walls of denial, there's nothing left to do but face the pain.

Many times denial is based on the false belief that *it must be my fault*. This is exactly what Roger thought. He perceived himself as having disobeyed his father. It never occurred to him that he did the best he could—his only reason for failing was that the task was too much for a ten year old. Roger never would have realized his father's behavior was abusive if a professional counselor hadn't pointed it out.

What About You?

Just like Roger, you're going to need to do some spying on yourself to successfully breach the walls of denial you've built around your empty love tank. As you work through this section, try to be completely honest and objective. Take a position outside yourself and assess what kinds of abuses might have taken place in your childhood. Put a check by any of the abuses that apply to you.

1. ____ **Physical Abuse** involves spankings or beatings where bruises or other signs of physical distress result. Parents make little or no attempt to control their rage, giving full vent to their anger during punishment.
2. ____ **Emotional Abuse** takes place when a child is expected to take on adult roles and responsibilities prematurely. In

these cases the child often becomes a confidante or caretaker for the parents.

3. _____ **Sexual Abuse** happens when a child is used by an adult as a sexual object. This may involve the use of pictures, touching and fondling, or intercourse.

4. _____ **Mental Abuse** occurs when parents make statements that demean and belittle the child. It often involves swearing, blaming, and saying things like "You're no good" or "You'll never amount to anything."

Children almost always find a way to blame themselves for their parents' abuses. In Roger's case, he blamed himself for not getting his crew to finish the required jobs. In what ways did you blame yourself for the abuses you experienced?

I felt that it was my fault because I *(for instance, should have been*

quieter and more obedient) _____

_____

_____

Can you stop blaming yourself and accept the fact that you did not *make* your parents behave in an abusive manner?

_____ yes _____ no

Internalized Messages about Denial

The cycle of denial is communicated to the child by the parents, either directly or indirectly. Check the messages you received as a child that taught you to deny what was going on in your home.

1. _____ Don't say anything negative about our family to anyone.
2. _____ Don't ever let us look bad in front of others.

3. _____ No matter how much you hate us, never tell anyone.
4. _____ Keep that bruise covered, and don't tell anyone how you got it.

What kinds of indirect messages about denial did you receive from your parents? *(For instance, my parents taught me how to use half-truths to cover things up. My mother denied that the bruises on her arm were put there by my father. No one in my family was honest about his feelings of pain.)*

1. _____

_____

_____

2. _____

_____

_____

3. _____

_____

_____

All of these messages taught me that *(for instance, things weren't really as bad as they seemed; keeping a good face on the situation was the best way to cope. I should hide my feelings)*

_____

_____

Do you still believe these messages today? _____ yes _____ no

One way to overcome denial is to counter these lies with the truth. Be very honest with yourself as you finish these statements.

To an outsider we looked like a happy family, but the truth is *(for instance, there was a terrible conflict in our home)*

_____

_____

I have always thought that my parents did a good job of raising me, but the truth is *(for instance, I really suffered under their rageaholism; I got very little nurturance and love)*

_____

_____

I grew up thinking that the bad things happening in our home were my fault, but the truth is *(for instance, that I was a helpless victim of my father's problem with alcohol)*

_____

_____

Characteristics of a Person in Denial

People in denial typically show some of the characteristics listed below. Read through the explanations and check the statements that apply to you.

1. **Has difficulty with authority.** The fear you experienced in dealing with an abusive parent may transfer to people in authority over you now—your boss, pastor, a police officer, teacher, or counselor. This behavior is usually an overreaction, signaling oversensitivity or rebellion.

_____ I don't like people who are in charge of me.

_____ It's difficult for me to deal with my boss/pastor/teacher.

2. **Seeks approval.** You're always looking for ways to gain the approval of those you admire. You may buy them expensive gifts, give verbal compliments, and put tremendous effort into finding ways to please them. You put too much emphasis on gaining their approval.

_____ My main concern is making sure other people are happy.

_____ I just can't cope with life unless I have the approval of

(name the people) _____

_____

3. **Is easily victimized.** You don't protect yourself from others and often feel helpless and unable to put up any opposition. You can't say no, even if you feel you should. You're an easy target for salespeople.

_____ I feel as though people often take advantage of me.

_____ I often wish I had the backbone to say what I'm really thinking.

4. **Victimizes others.** It doesn't bother you to take advantage of people for your own selfish gain. You're basically self-centered and don't see other people's needs as important.

_____ It doesn't bother me to push people around a little.

_____ I feel that people who don't look out for themselves deserve whatever comes their way.

5. **Is attracted to unhealthy relationships.** You never seem to learn how to choose the right friends. You have experienced repeated failures in relationships with abusive or alcoholic partners or spouses.

_____ I know being with _(name the person)_ _____

is bad for me, but I can't help myself.

_____ I can begin to see a bad pattern in my relationships with significant other people, but I fear I may not be able to change the pattern.

6. **Is unable to be assertive.** You are unable to express negative thoughts to others. You couldn't send back a burnt steak in a restaurant. You are a silent sufferer and keep your feelings to yourself.

_____ I consider myself to be painfully shy.

_____ I seldom express my opinion, especially if I feel others won't agree with me.

7. **Is unable to express feelings.** You like to keep your distance in a relationship. You tend to stay on an intellectual level with people, talking about thoughts and ideas, but never really connecting heart-to-heart.

_____ I think, but I don't feel.

_____ I don't really know what I feel.

8. **Is terrified of abandonment.** You believe that anyone you love will eventually leave you. You're always looking for signs that others don't like you or aren't including you.

_____ I always interpret what others say about me in the most negative way.

_____ My greatest fear is of being left alone.

9. **Feels a great deal of guilt.** You take responsibility for what happens to others, even if you have absolutely no control over situations. You feel that you should always be trying to make things right. You're constantly finding ways to blame yourself.

_____ I'm always worrying about what happens to significant others in my life.

_____ I'm always thinking of ways to intervene in the lives of those who are closest to me.

10. **Feels the past is best forgotten.** You don't see any value in discussing your past in the light of current problems. You doubt that your early experiences had much impact on what's happening in your life today.

_____ I just want to get on with life and forget about the past.
_____ I feel impatient with people who want to probe into my childhood.

Did you identify with any of these ten characteristics?
_____ yes _____ no

If you recognized some of these attitudes and behaviors in yourself, it's time to acknowledge that *you do these things because you are in pain.* Denial is what you began to use as a child to help avoid the pain. But the hard fact is that you will not make any progress toward healing as long as you continue on your path of denial. By continuing in these behaviors, you are actually intensifying your pain. Denial served its purpose in your childhood— it helped you survive. Now you are an adult capable of analytical thinking. You can understand your parents, face your childhood pain, and move ahead toward resolving these issues.

How has living in denial helped you survive the abuse in your past? *(For instance, I have learned how to work hard in order to please my superiors. I learned how to be independent and look out for myself.)*

_____

_____

How has living in denial hurt you? *(For instance, I'm treating my children the same way my parents treated me. I have a hard time trusting anyone.)*

_____

_____

GIVE YOURSELF PERMISSION

Your codependent behavior has you trapped and miserable. In order to release yourself from the trap, you must turn off your strong denial system. It is painful, but the reality of being trapped for a lifetime is a worse fate. Give yourself permission right now to identify the issues from the past that have contributed to your unhealthy behaviors.

I, _____, do hereby give myself permission to face the pain from my past. I acknowledge that I am breaking the rules I learned as a child in my family of origin. I purposely break those rules, knowing that they have not helped me develop into a healthy person. I will not, however, use this newfound freedom to hurt or blame significant others in my life.

I humbly give myself permission to become a healthy person.

Signed _____

Date _____

Congratulations! You have just made a commitment to reverse the denial cycle. It may be painful for you right now, but it's a very important step in your recovery.

THOUGHT CHECK

One thing I've done that I can feel good about is _____

_____

_____

I need to follow up on _____

_____

An important new insight I've gained is that _____

5. WHEN THE LID COMES OFF

Mary grew up in a home where her parents never argued or expressed negative feelings toward each other. After her marriage she felt terribly guilty about being angry with her husband, Bill. It didn't take Bill long to discover how easily he could take advantage of his wife. He didn't really understand that it was Mary's fear of her own anger that made her so compliant, but he sure enjoyed "having his cake and eating it too." Everything was going well for Bill; he had total control of the finances, had no responsibilities at home, and could spend his leisure time any way he desired. While Bill was having a heyday, Mary sank deeper and deeper into depression.

Anger is a legitimate and necessary emotion. That's a hard statement for many people to accept, because they don't understand the positive aspects of anger. Extremes of anger—either hidden or uncontrolled—are negative and destructive. This chapter will help you recognize how you deal with anger and offer some positive alternatives.

Mary is an example of a person with hidden anger. She always felt guilty about being angry and came to view herself as a bad person. The fact is that no one is immune from anger. Mary had numerous experiences of legitimate anger that she simply repressed and tried to hide. Repressing anger doesn't solve any problems—in fact, it creates more. Repressed anger will often surface as depression. It also emerges in passive-aggressive behaviors—like when a perfectionistic wife keeps scorching her husband's shirts even though she knows perfectly well how to iron. The unconscious action of scorching the shirt provides an outlet for her anger. Anxiety and panic attacks are other examples of how repressed anger might express itself.

The effects of uncontrolled anger are equally damaging. Mental and physical abuse usually occur when parents cut loose and express violent, uncontrolled anger. It's true that children can be very frustrating, and parents may have legitimate reasons for becoming angry. But it is never right to express rage at others abusively.

Uncontrolled anger is what most people imagine when they think of the word *anger*. A patient named Betty said she would never allow herself to feel anger because she didn't want to be anything like her father, who beat her during his rages. Betty needed to learn that anger can be a good thing when it's expressed positively, and it can help bring a problem to resolution.

In order to understand your attitude toward anger and how you deal with it, you'll need to look back on what you learned from your family of origin.

Expressing anger in my family:

1. _____ was taboo.
2. _____ was seen as a sign of weakness.
3. _____ was something only adults could do.
4. _____ almost always involved violence and destruction.

My mother expressed her anger by *(for instance, clamming up and giving everyone the cold treatment; slamming doors)*

_____

_____

_____

_____

My father expressed his anger by *(for instance, yelling at us; slapping people around)*

_____

_____

_____

_____

When I expressed anger as a child I *(for instance, threw tantrums; hid in a closet and cried)*

_____

_____

_____

_____

My parents responded to my anger by *(for instance, yelling at me; sending me to my room)*

_____

_____

_____

_____

I began to believe that anger *(for instance, was always wrong; would always make things worse)*

_____

_____

_____

_____

How has your family's expression of anger affected your current expression of anger? *(For instance, my parents were rageaholics; now I don't feel or express anger.)*

My parents _____

_____;

now I _____

_____

When someone gets angry with me I *(for instance, usually think they're right; just try to get out of the way)*

_____

_____

We all face situations every day that stir up feelings of anger. Some situations are more intense than others, but at least one irritating event happens to everyone each day. Replay the last three days in your mind. List five things that made you angry. *(For instance, someone took the parking spot I was waiting for. My friend didn't call when she said she would.)*

1. _____

2. _____

3. _____

4. _____

5. _____

Is it hard for you to remember the things that made you angry?
_____ yes _____ no

Can you imagine anger without violence?   _____ yes _____ no

What might happen if you fully acknowledge your anger? *(For instance, I might get out of control and never calm down; I would act just like Dad did; it wouldn't change anything.)*

_____

_____

_____

_____

Taking a New Look at Old Resentments

Resentment is not as simple as it may seem. Like a multi-skinned onion, resentment hides multilayers of emotions that must be peeled back and exposed before healing can begin.

- Beneath resentment is the *anger* that your needs are not being met.
- Beneath anger is usually *hurt* that your needs are not being met.
- Beneath hurt, at the deepest core, is *fear* that your needs will never be met.

Until you inventory these resentments and truly understand the deeper anger and fears that underlie them, they will fester like emotional toxic waste. Think about that statement for a moment: You can take toxic waste and put it in drums . . . you can try to contain it . . . you can bury it underground . . . but over months and years it will begin to bleed through and poison the environment.

The same thing happens with the resentments you hold. That's why it's so important to grapple with how you've been hurt by others and begin to make peace with that. One way to make peace with the fear and the hurt is to see the people who have hurt you as fellow sufferers. You need to realize that they are hurting, just as you are.

The first step is to peel back the layers and reveal the vulnerable, tender heart of fear that exists at the very core of every resentment or grudge you hold.

Name five people who are objects of your anger or resentment, either presently or from your past.

1. _____

2. _____

3. _____

4. _____

5. _____

Let's work through some thoughts about these five resentments you've just listed. Examples of how Mary, the repressed wife at the beginning of this chapter, would complete these statements will show you what to do.

(Mary's answers)
I have resented ___*my younger brother Tom.*___

I was angry because ___*he always rebelled against my parents and*___

*went his own way.*___

I was hurt because ___*I was actually jealous that my parents still*___

*loved and accepted him even though he didn't do things the way*___ *they wanted him to.*

My hurt may have stemmed from the fear that *I really wanted to rebel and be like my brother, but I was afraid that they would reject me if I did.*

Now complete these same statements about your resentments.

1. I have resented _____

   I was angry because _____

   _____

   I was hurt because _____

   _____

   My hurt may have stemmed from the fear that _____

   _____

2. I have resented _____

   I was angry because _____

   _____

   I was hurt because _____

   My hurt may have stemmed from the fear that _____

   _____

3. I have resented _____

   I was angry because _____

I was hurt because _____

My hurt may have stemmed from the fear that _____

4. I have resented _____

I was angry because _____

I was hurt because _____

My hurt may have stemmed from the fear that _____

5. I have resented _____

I was angry because _____

I was hurt because _____

My hurt may have stemmed from the fear that _____

I tell myself that expressing my anger with these people:

_____ would be wrong.

_____ would only make our relationship worse.

_____ wouldn't do any good.

I believe that my anger:

_____ should be ignored, because the Christian thing to do is turn the other cheek.

_____ will eventually go away.

It's very important for you to learn to accept the fact that anger is a legitimate human emotion. Many people feel that if they expressed anger they would be displeasing God. This is simply not true! God vented His anger toward the wayward Israelites. Jesus showed anger on several occasions. Anger expressed appropriately can be a very good thing. Expressed inappropriately, it can be a dangerously destructive emotion. Check the issues on this list that apply to the way you express anger.

1. _____ I always acknowledge—at least to myself—that I am angry, and I think about how and when to share my feelings with someone else.

2. _____ I scream at whoever happens to be nearby when I am angry.

3. _____ I try my best never to be angry.

4. _____ When I get angry I give the person the cold shoulder.

5. _____ When I am angry with someone I get back at him or her in little ways, like doing something I know the person doesn't like and then saying it was a mistake.

6. _____ I accept my anger as a natural response to disappointment and express it, but don't let myself get out of control.

7. _____ When someone makes me angry I "let them have it."

8. _____ I just try to do better when I am angry.

9. _____ I never say anything to the people who anger me, but I sometimes enjoy frustrating them in return.

10. _____ I don't tell people I'm mad at them; I just get them back in subtle ways.

11. _____ I rarely let my anger get out of control, but sometimes it catches me off guard.

12. _____ I can't control myself when I am angry.

13. _____ When I'm angry I try to figure out what I've done wrong to cause my anger.

14. _____ I never get angry, but sometimes other people get irritated with me.

15. _____ I have secretly done nasty things to people I'm angry with—like letting the air out of their tires.

16. _____ I think of anger as just one of a number of healthy emotions.

17. _____ I blow up easily.

18. _____ I'm never angry at other people; I just get angry with myself.

19. _____ I may purposely be late for an appointment with someone who angers me.

20. _____ I joke about sensitive topics with people I don't like.

21. _____ I'm not afraid of my anger.

22. _____ I usually feel guilty when I yell at others, but I don't apologize.

23. _____ I am always to blame when there is anger involved.

24. _____ I gossip about people I'm angry with.

25. _____ I love to hear that people I don't like are having troubles.

26. _____ I have worked through anger and come up with positive results many times.

27. _____ I'm uptight and angry most of the time.

28. _____ I cut myself, take pills, or binge when I'm angry.

29. _____ I put off doing things for people I resent, even though I get to them eventually.

30. _____ I don't get mad—I get even.

We have put the responses from the list above into groups that signify a specific pattern in dealing with anger. To identify your pattern, circle the numbers of the responses you checked in the groups below.

A. Numbers 1, 6, 11, 16, 21, and 26 show appropriate anger. This indicates that you fully acknowledge your anger to yourself and choose to express it in ways that take your feelings and the feelings of others into account.

B. Numbers 2, 7, 12, 17, 22, and 27 reflect uncontrolled anger. You make little or no effort to control yourself when you're angry, so you end up hurting others and yourself. Many times your anger leads you to destructive relationships.

C. Numbers 3, 8, 13, 18, 23, and 28 indicate repressed anger. Hidden and repressed anger usually surface in bad feelings toward yourself. It is destructive because it limits relationships and creates further problems, like depression and illness.

D. Numbers 4, 9, 14, 19, 24, and 29 evidence passive or passive/aggressive patterns. You do not openly acknowledge your anger, but you get back at others in subtle ways. You remain anonymous, but the person you're angry with does experience the consequences of your anger. This is not as self-destructive as repressed anger, but it does severely limit healthy relationships.

E. Numbers 5, 10, 15, 20, 25, and 30 show aggressive-passive/aggressive anger. You still remain anonymous, as in category D. The only difference is that you are more aggressive in the anonymous ways you express your anger. You do things that are designed to hurt the person you're angry with.

In which category did you circle the most responses?

A ـــــ   B ـــــ   C ـــــ   D ـــــ   E ـــــ

Use a star to indicate where you would place yourself on the continuum of anger on the next page.

Continuum of Anger

A. Hidden	B. PA	C. Appropriate	D. PA	E. Rage
Repressed	Passive	Anger	Aggressive	Uncontrolled

Read over the description of that category once again. Do you agree that this identifies the way you deal with anger?

_____ yes _____ no

If you are on either side of the continuum, you need to make it your goal to move toward the center, toward finding the right balance in expressing your anger and taking into account other people's feelings.

Why do you express anger the way you do? *(For instance, this is the pattern I learned from my mother.)*

_____

_____

Anger is a healthy emotion. Learning to express it in positive, constructive ways is an important key to your mental health. Check the statements that you choose to incorporate in your recovery.

1. _____ I'm not going to hide my angry feelings anymore.
2. _____ I'm committed to learning to control my rage.
3. _____ I'm open to learning better ways of expressing my anger.
4. _____ If I say that I never get angry, I'm just deceiving myself.
5. _____ I now realize that anger can sometimes be a good thing.

How Can I Express Anger Appropriately?

The first step is to understand how the emotion of anger works. When something makes you angry, the first thing you feel is a rush of adrenaline. It's wise to have some kind of positive physical outlet for that first emotional surge, so that you don't lose control. Some people find it very helpful to take a brisk walk. List some positive outlets you could use to deal with anger and keep yourself from raging at another person or hurting yourself.

When I feel a surge of anger I could *(for instance, hit a pillow, write a letter that I don't plan to mail explaining all my feelings, scrub the kitchen floor)*

1. _____

2. _____

3. _____

4. _____

5. _____

It's very likely that repressed or inappropriately expressed anger is a part of your codependency. Think of someone you're angry with. Use these pages to write that person a letter that fully expresses your rage. You can safely give full vent to your feelings, because you won't be sending the letter.

If someone has abused you or is abusing you now, write your letter to that person. It may be someone from your past who is no longer living. You may even want to write more than one letter.

Dear _____,

_____

_____

_____

_____

_____

_____

_____

_____

_____

_____

_____

_____

_____

_____

_____

_____

Sincerely, _____

Circle the word that shows how you felt about writing the letter(s).

good   scared   angry   hurt   confused

Would you consider rewriting the letter in a milder tone and sending it? _____ yes _____ no

Forgiveness

The next step in the healing process is to grant forgiveness to those who have hurt you. Bitterness results when repressed or unforgiven anger sours in your heart. Bitterness robs you of enjoying life and gives the person you are angry with power over you.

Use these lines to tell what forgiveness means to you.

_____

_____

_____

Have you ever felt genuine peace after forgiving someone?
_____ yes _____ no

Many of the patients we work with have a hard time with the issue of forgiveness. Janine, for example, felt all kinds of red flags go up when anyone mentioned forgiveness. She couldn't understand how forgiving could be of any value. She thought that forgiving her stepfather would somehow excuse the sexual abuse she had suffered from him.

Many people share Janine's misunderstanding. Forgiveness is not just for the guilty person. It's for your own sake, for your mental health. Forgiveness helps you say to the people who have wronged you, "You no longer have power to hurt me; I will not let rage and bitterness against you ruin my life." Forgiveness is not an emotion. It is a decision to follow God's direction and obey Him. It's a choice, not a feeling. Some people fear that granting forgiveness will make them a victim again. This is not true. When you choose to forgive you are doing so from a position of strength. True forgiveness is a careful process that involves acknowledging rage, revoking revenge, and accepting forgiveness as a God-given solution to your anger.

Earlier in this chapter you listed five people who are objects of your anger or resentment. In the spaces below, write the names of those you have not completely forgiven.

1. _____

2. _____

3. _____

4. _____

5. _____

THE STEPS OF FORGIVENESS

Read over this explanation of the forgiveness process. Then identify where you are in the process with each of the five people above by writing the appropriate number by their names.

1. Acknowledge the full extent of the wrong. Confront any denial you may harbor about what this person has done to make you angry.
2. Acknowledge the full extent of your anger, both toward yourself and toward the other person.
3. Grieve out this old anger by expressing it in appropriate settings such as support group meetings.
4. Choose to let go of the need for revenge. Resolve that carrying bitterness and anger only gives that person power to hurt you. Accept God's design for forgiveness as the antidote to bitterness.
5. Reestablish the relationship. If the person asks forgiveness, forgive him or her; if not, decide what kind of relationship, if any, you can have with that person.

Forgiveness works in a cycle: First God in His grace forgives us; then we, in turn, forgive others. We need God's grace to accomplish the task. Old resentments are hard to let go of, but they can block the flow of grace in our lives and prevent healing. Now is the time to forgive.

Heavenly Father, I know that you have graciously

forgiven me. Please give me the grace to forgive *(write in names)* _____ in return. Please open the channels of love that have been blocked by anger and resentment. Amen.

THOUGHT CHECK

One thing that I've done that I can feel good about is _____

_____

_____

I need to follow up on _____

_____

_____

An important new insight I've gained is that _____

_____

_____

_____

6. LITTLE KID LOST

You have faced the reality of abuse in your life. Now it's time to clarify and work through it. The abuses you experienced as a child can create the phenomenon we call *lost childhood*. Those unmet emotional needs at the bottom layer of the four-tier cake mean that you were robbed of some significant nurturance as a child. You had to grow up too fast.

Roger's situation is a classic case of lost childhood. You will recall that at age ten he was forced to manage a group of migrant workers with whom he could barely communicate. The group was given a demanding work load, and Roger was held personally accountable for any shortcomings. His father screamed at him, berated him, and beat him with a leather belt when the group failed to perform according to expectations. Those responsibilities would have been difficult for a mature teenager to handle. Roger never had a chance to be a kid.

In order to understand how this phenomenon of lost childhood affected you, we are going to focus on the third layer of the cake—the abuse layer. In previous chapters we have touched on abuse. Now we're going to ask you to specifically identify the various kinds of abuse you experienced as a child. It's very important for you to realize at this point that we are not talking about legal definitions. Roger, a lawyer acquainted with family law, could not see that the treatment he received as a child was abusive, even though it would have been considered so in a court of law. He was blind to the fact that those laws applied to his situation.

We all suffer different degrees of abuse. It is important not to discount your particular abuse by comparing it to someone else's experience. You are not doing this workbook for someone else—you are doing it for yourself. Even subtle abuse is damaging, whether or not it would be classified as abuse in court.

Understand, too, that these forms of abuse do not cause irreversible damage. Joseph (of the coat-of-many-colors fame) in the book of Genesis was a victim of abuse. His mother died during his childhood; his father doted on him overprotectively; his brothers hated him and said so. They sold him into slavery, and he suffered for years. And yet, when the tables were turned, Joseph was strong enough to forgive his brothers and welcome his father.

Not all of us are as strong or as fortunate as Joseph was. Most people will have better lives and healthier relationships if they deal with the unhappy issues from their childhood. There is a healing process. One of the first steps in that process is to identify the factors that prevented your love tank from being adequately filled.

In chapter 3 you were asked to identify types of abuse that occurred in your home. Perhaps you didn't check any of those categories because you didn't think that what happened to you was serious enough to be called abuse. Let's take a closer look at some specific abuses and see how they may have contributed to your lost childhood. Realize that one form of abuse may breed another, and several types of abuse may grow concurrently. As you read through the descriptions of abuse below, highlight or underline anything that describes how you were treated as a child. Then check off the specific statements that apply to you.

A. Active abuse is very up front and easy to see. It includes verbal violence, battering, beating, and sexual molestation. Manifestations of extreme anger or rage are harmful and destructive, but not necessarily illegal. Sexual activity with children is illegal in nearly all venues.

_____ When my parents physically punished me, I sometimes came away with bruises.

_____ One or both of my parents was chemically dependent.

_____ I can remember my parents yelling and swearing at me, and saying things like, "You'll never amount to anything."

_____ My parents didn't provide adequate nutrition—I was sometimes left to scrounge food for myself.

_____ My parents did not provide a sheltered, nurturing environment—I never really felt safe and cared for.

_____ I was forced to look at sexually provocative material with one of my parents.

_____ One of my parents touched me in unhealthy ways that made me feel dirty and used.

_____ One of my parents always spoke in a loud, critical voice.

B. **Passive abuse** is more subtle and harder to detect, but can have equally damaging effects on children. Passive abuse is characterized by a lack of parental emotional involvement and investment in the life of a child. It may spring from several parental problems, including workaholism, perfectionism, depression, emotional coldness, a troubled marriage, divorce, or death. (The inclusion of death and divorce here is not meant to be judgmental; the reality is that these events do affect children deeply. This must be recognized and dealt with accordingly.) One or both parents may be so preoccupied that he or she is not available to the child emotionally, physically, or both. Unfortunately, many very damaging forms of passive abuse—like workaholism or perfectionism—are never identified as such. In fact, they may be praised and idealized in some sections of society.

_____ One or both of my parents was a workaholic.

_____ My parents were divorced.

_____ I took care of myself (or other children) at an early age.

_____ My parents didn't take time to discipline me in any consistent manner.

_____ My parents weren't available for important events, like school programs.

_____ It seemed as if my parents paid more attention to the dog or the newspaper than they did to me.

_____ My parents seldom took time for significant conversations with me.

C. Emotional incest is when a parent relies on a child to fulfill adult-like roles. It's an extreme role reversal in which the child becomes a confidante or even a caretaker of the parent. It has nothing to do with sexual matters, although in extreme cases it can lead to incest of a sexual sort. The child may be expected to assume adult responsibilities, like cleaning, shopping, and caring for other children. Emotional incest is subtle, hard to identify, and usually involves intense denial—that's one reason we use such an attention-getting term to name it.

_____ I am the best friend of one or both of my parents.

_____ One or both parents lived their life dreams through me.

_____ One of my parents sometimes talked to me about things that made me uncomfortable.

_____ I took care of household duties my parents were unable to attend to.

_____ I felt the need to make my parents look good.

_____ I felt responsible for one or both of my parents' emotional well-being.

D. Unfinished business refers to a child's being expected to achieve the parents' unrealized goals. It might mean attending their alma mater, carrying on the family business, or fulfilling a secret desire that the parent was unable to do. Parents lay out certain expectations, hoping to enjoy vicariously the fruits of what the child accomplishes. This creates impossible expectations, because, in fact, the parents' need can never be satisified in this way. This abuse results in adult-children who tend to be depressed and dissatisfied, never having been given an opportunity to fulfill their individual needs and desires.

_____ I sometimes feel that my parents are living their life through me.

_____ I had to follow a certain path in life to help my parents resolve some issues in their lives.

_____ I've never really felt free to follow my own dreams.

_____ My parents used subtle messages to get me to follow their prescribed course for my life.

E. Negative existential messages come from parents who are not at peace with themselves or the world around them. Through direct or subtly expressed messages, the parent gives the child negative ideas about personal worth, the world, and life in general. These messages may be directed, as with the parent who says, "Why do I even bother with you?" or they may be picked up by the child who must live in an atmosphere of negativism and depression.

_____ My parent sometimes threatened to commit suicide.

_____ My parents seemed to be depressed and seldom demonstrated any joy in living.

_____ My parents saw the world as a bleak and hopeless place, and they never encouraged me to try to make things better.

_____ My parents frequently directed critical or accusatory statements toward me.

Summarize what kind of abuse happened to you as a child, and by whom.

Type of Abuse	_Abuser(s)_
_____ Active abuse	_____
_____ Passive abuse	_____
_____ Emotional incest	_____

_____ Unfinished business   _____

_____ Negative existential   _____
messages

PLEASURE/PAIN HISTORY

Another way to get in touch with your childhood is to complete a Pleasure/Pain History in which you review the events that had great impact on you.

What are your happiest memories from childhood? *(For instance, special birthdays, vacations, holidays, surprises.)*

1. _____

2. _____

3. _____

4. _____

What are your saddest memories from childhood? *(For instance, disappointments in sports or at school, hurtful statements made by parents or peers, times when you were lonely and hurt.)*

1. _____

2. _____

3. _____

4. _____

What do these events reveal about how you view yourself?
(For instance, my happiest times were when someone gave

me attention and was pleased with my behavior. My worst memories center around being hurt by someone I needed.)

_____

_____

_____

How did they lead you to codependent behavior? *(For instance, I learned that I needed to please people and make them happy in order to keep them from hurting me.)*

_____

_____

_____

Think about the relationship between you and your parents and siblings in your family of origin. How would you draw a portrait of your family as you saw it as a child? Would you be standing beside your mom or your dad? Or would you be sitting off in a corner by yourself? Would one of your siblings be closer to your parents? Who would be closest to you? What was the relationship between your mom and dad like? Would they be looking at each other? Would their backs be turned on each other? Would they be fighting? Would you or one of your brothers or sisters be standing between your parents, trying to stop the fighting?

Use simple stick figures to draw a portrait of your family as you remember it as a child. Don't worry about your art work; instead, concentrate on capturing the feelings and dynamics between people.

Where are you in the picture? *(For instance, over in the corner by myself; taking center stage; trying to keep everyone happy.)*

_____

_____

What kind of child were you? *(For instance, sensitive and quiet; energetic; happy and bubbly.)*

_____

_____

What characteristics of your family stand out in the picture? *(For instance, my parents were not together; we were all into our own things—Dad had alcohol, Mom had her work, my sister had to make straight A's.)*

_____

_____

_____

All children need a trusted, caring adult who will act as a sounding board when disturbing events and major questions about life come up. When parents, for one reason or another, don't fulfill this need, children feel emotionally abandoned. They have to grow up quickly and face these issues on their own, without nurturance or comfort. This forced maturity can contribute greatly to the issue of a lost childhood.

Do you remember being afraid to share important secrets or questions with your parents, because you felt they couldn't handle what you wanted to ask them?   _____ yes _____ no

What were some of those secrets or questions? *(For instance, I wanted to ask questions about sexuality after I played doctor with my friend. When my mother went to the hospital I was afraid she was going to die, but I knew I would be ridiculed if I asked about it.)*

1. _____

   _____

2. _____

   _____

3. _____

   _____

Describe some of the situations that robbed you of your childhood. In what ways were you forced to grow up too fast? *(For instance, I was always busy worrying about my parents, acting as a marriage counselor. I had to assume responsibility for my younger siblings. I was a latchkey kid at a very early age.)*

_____

_____

_____

One way you can begin to heal those lost childhood hurts is to write a letter that speaks to your childhood self. In the letter, express the kind of comfort and understanding you wished your parents had given. Talk about understanding your hurts and loneliness. Give encouragement; mention your dreams and hopes. Become for yourself the caring parent you never had.

As a Parent

If you are a parent, dealing with your lost childhood brings up other issues for you. You may find yourself denying the abuse you experienced because acknowledging it would make you face the ways you are abusing your children. If you are going to become the parent your children need, you will need to deal very honestly with yourself on this score. Don't let yourself feel hopeless or overwhelmed. Although you can't change the past, you can change the future.

What issues came up for you as a parent during this exercise? *(For instance, I see that I'm putting pressure on my kids to do things I was never able to do.)*

1. _____

2. _____

3. _____

Do you see yourself trying to live your childhood through your children? _____ yes _____ no

Are some of your behaviors denying your children their childhood? _____ yes _____ no

In what ways? *(For instance, I'm relying too much on Danny to listen to my problems and give me advice.)*

1. _____

2. _____

3. _____

List three concerns you have about yourself as a parent. *(For instance, when I discipline the kids I let them feel*

the full force of my rage; I realize that I'm creating an
atmosphere of depression and hopelessness.)

1. _____

2. _____

3. _____

Now think about how you could change your behavior to take care
of those concerns. *(For instance, I could send the kids to their
rooms while I get my anger under control. I can realize how
much my attitude affects my children and get help for myself.)*

1. _____

2. _____

3. _____

Many people who suffer from a lost childhood have difficulty enjoying
leisure activities and play. Getting in touch with the fun-loving carefree side of
yourself is a significant part of the healing process. You may need to learn to
play for the first time! It's important to see that taking time to play brings an
emotional balance to your life, and it can be a source of strength in this
difficult healing period.

What were the things you most liked to do as a child?
*(For instance, color and paint, play outdoors, jump rope,
climb trees, shoot baskets.)*

1. _____

2. _____

3. _____

4. _____

5. _____

Put a star beside two of these favorite activities and go do them.
Then describe how this experience made you feel. *(For instance,
I was surprised at how much I enjoyed coloring; I felt really
energized after shooting some baskets.)*

1. _____

_____

2. _____

_____

Play and leisure are important parts of being healthy and need to
be a regular part of your life. When will you schedule your next
play session, and what will you do? *(For instance, I will take the
family roller-skating on Friday night.)*

_____

_____

THOUGHT CHECK

One thing that I've done that I can feel good about is _____

_____

_____

I need to follow up on _____

_____

_____

An important new insight I've gained is that _____

_____

_____

_____

7. BAD PENNIES

Roger sat in the counseling office, remembering his father. He asked, "Why should I care about my father and what he thinks of me? He's a rage-aholic and an abuser, and he never gave me anything. I had to earn every penny and every belonging I ever received for as long as I can remember. Why in the world would I want to go home?"

You may have asked yourself that same question countless times. You may wonder what makes you keep seeking the approval of people who made you feel as a child that you were never quite good enough. The reality is that everyone has an irresistible homing instinct. Why we do is a question that goes beyond human reason.

The homing instinct is not geographic—it operates totally within our minds. It may seem on the surface that we have given up on our family of origin, but in reality we often seek to reconstruct it in our present lives. We find ways to bring back our childhood home. Like a bad penny, the same negative situations turn up in our lives over and over again. We all possess a primal need to re-create our original family situation, even if it was destructive and painful. This repetition compulsion is one of the most baffling things a codependent person has to come to terms with.

The following drawing activity will help you to discover how the repetition compulsion is at work in your life. In the house on the left, write the negative situations that went on in your family of origin. In the house on the right, write about the negative situations that are happening in your current family setting. If you live alone, write out the negative issues that you personally face.

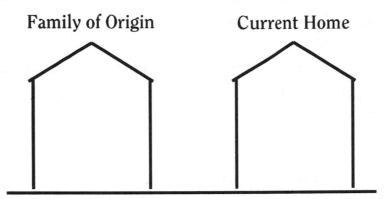

Family of Origin   **Current Home**

Can you identify the repetition compulsion in your drawings?
_____ yes _____ no

List the negative elements that appear in both households. *(For instance, my dad became physically violent when he was angry with me, and now I am physically violent with my children.)*

1. _____

_____

2. _____

_____

3. _____

_____

Do you see a similarity between your spouse and your mother or father? _____ yes _____ no

Can you acknowledge that you may have married someone similar to one of your parents so that you could finally get her or him to love you? _____ yes _____ no

Have you gotten the approval you've been longing for? _____ yes _____ no

When you fight with your spouse, do you fight in the same way your parents did? _____ yes _____ no

Do you not fight at all because of their fighting, or lack of fighting? _____ yes _____ no

Magical Thinking

Magical thinking is the belief all children develop that says, "If I do such-and-such, my parents will love me." As a child you couldn't understand that Mommy and Daddy had problems of their own. You perceived that everything that went wrong in your home was your fault. Magical thinking is an outgrowth of that fallacy, often characterized by *if only* statements. *If only I had stayed quietly out of the way, Daddy wouldn't have slapped me around. If only I could get better grades, Mommy would be pleased with me.*

Go back inside your mind as a child. What was some of the magical thinking that went on inside your head? *(For instance, if only I were better at sports, Dad would be proud of me.)*

_____

_____

_____

_____

Magical thinking does not disappear with childhood. Codependent adults still carry around the same magical thoughts. They are damaging because they cause you to take responsibility for every negative situation, and they build up false hopes, creating repeated disappointments in your life.

It's quite possible that much of your adult behavior is motivated by magical thinking. What are some of the magical thoughts that have carried over from your childhood? *(For instance, if only I could be thinner, people would find me attractive. If only I can earn this advanced degree, my father will respect me.)*

1. _____

_____

2. _____

_____

3. _____

_____

I can see how these thoughts are damaging because *(for instance, I've been thin before, and it didn't solve all my problems. I would be getting a degree just to get Dad's approval, and I'll be frustrated and exhausted)*

1. _____

_____

2. _____

_____

3. _____

_____

Guilt

Everyone experiences guilt quite naturally and justifiably. We don't have to *try* to feel guilty. You don't have to argue the validity of original sin to find genuine guilt, even in a small child. True guilt can be resolved. The normal transgressions of childhood, like sneaking cookies without permission, are obvious—they can be forgiven. False guilt, like children blaming themselves for their parents' divorce, is not as easily detected. It galls. It eats. Years later, unnoticed and unforgiven, it may surface in unpredictable ways.

Many people describe their guilt as a large, heavy bag they drag around behind them. Can you envision such a bag?

Identify the guilt you carry with you by writing it inside the bag below. It is important to use a pencil for this exercise so that you'll be able to erase things later. *(For instance, you might include guilt from a divorce, that you're gaining weight, that you don't please everyone at work, that you can't make everyone in your family happy, that your children have problems in school.)*

YOUR PAST

Now go back inside your childhood mind. What kind of guilt do you remember? Draw it in the bag below. *(For instance, you might remember stealing candy, cheating on a test, making your parents angry, or not being able to get along with siblings.)*

TRUE GUILT

It's time to sort out your guilt bags. You are morally responsible for those behaviors that are in violation of God's laws. Marital infidelity, lying about items on your expense account, and cheating on income taxes are examples of moral guilt. You can rid yourself of that guilt by confessing those things to God and accepting the forgiveness He promises.

Read over the Bible verse below. Circle the part that tells what you are supposed to do. Underline the words that explain God's response.

If we confess our sins, He is faithful and just to forgive us our sins and to cleanse us from all unrighteousness. (1 John 1:9)

After you have asked God's forgiveness, go back and erase those things from your guilt bags.

FALSE GUILT

The items that remain in your bags after you have confessed your sins to God can be classified as false guilt. These feelings are often the residue of unhealthy relationships. It's time to give those false guilt feelings back to the people who laid them on you in the first place. For each item left in your guilt bags, name the person the guilt really belongs to. Write the names below, then erase the items from your guilt bag.

I'm giving my false guilt back to *(for instance, my mother for making me feel guilty when she screamed at me; my older brother for making me feel guilty when he made me look at his pornography)*

1. _____

_____

2. _____

_____

3. _____

_____

You may need help with this step. We have found that people who struggle with guilt sometimes have a hard time discerning what is authentic guilt and what is actually false guilt. Ask a counselor, pastor, or trusted friend to go over your list and help you recognize those items for which you need to ask God's forgiveness.

Do you have an empty guilt bag? _____ yes _____ no

You can, if you release the legacy of false guilt and surrender authentic guilt to God's grace.

YOUR PRESENT

The repetition compulsion sometimes surfaces when people choose a marriage partner. Many people pick a spouse who in some way resembles their mother or father. Most commonly the adult child will marry a person who emotionally resembles or re-creates some dynamic with the parent of the opposite sex. But it can be the parent of the same sex. Some people reverse this procedure by looking for a spouse who demonstrates exactly the opposite characteristics of one of their parents.

Did you marry (or date) someone who resembled one of your parents? _____ yes _____ no

Which one? _____ mother _____ father

If you answered no to the above question, is your spouse the exact opposite of one of your parents? _____ yes _____ no

Which one? _____ mother _____ father

Describe how your spouse reflects similar or opposite characteristics of the parent you checked. *(For instance, my father was emotionally distant, but my husband is warm and supportive. My mother was rigid and domineering, and so is my wife.)*

_____

_____

_____

Look for a similar pattern in other past or present relationships. Are there close friends who strongly remind you of one of your parents? _____ yes _____ no

Write their names and similar characteristics.

	Name	*Characteristic*
1.	_____	_____
2.	_____	_____
3.	_____	_____

If you are in a new family with young children, do you sometimes see your children reacting to you in the same way you responded to your parents? _____ yes _____ no

List three situations in your present family that are similar to memories of your childhood. *(For instance, my dad was stern and authoritative, and now my husband is the same way with me and our children. There was a lot of underlying tension in my childhood home, and I can feel that same tension in my present home.)*

1. _____

_____

2. _____

_____

3. _____

_____

Before you get off track and decide you need to focus on your children or your spouse to repair the damage you may have repeated—stop! That will come in time. These questions have been designed to make you aware of what is really going on in your family system. Now you know that the repetition compulsion is something you need to contend with.

But don't jump the gun. It's essential at this point to concentrate on *your* healing. You have discovered that the same mistakes happen again and again. Getting things right in your life is the first step in making things right in your family. Now that we've raised these issues, we're ready to launch into the ten stages of recovery. The coming chapters will help you to learn how to stop the powerful repetition compulsion from hurting you and your family.

THOUGHT CHECK

One thing that I've done that I can feel good about is _____

_____

_____

I need to follow up on _____

_____

_____

An important new insight I've gained is that _____

_____

_____

_____

PART TWO

THE TEN STAGES OF RECOVERY

8. EXPLORATION AND DISCOVERY

You have learned a great deal about many issues that have exposed the causes of your codependency—love tanks, denial, anger, lost childhood, and the repetition compulsion. Part two of this workbook will discuss the ten stages of recovery, which are also found in *Love Is a Choice*. Each stage represents a step in putting your life back together, a healing from the pain that created your codependency.

In *Love Is a Choice* we compared going through these healing stages to riding a roller coaster. You climb, climb, climb—then suddenly the bottom drops out. It seems like a long trip down before things begin to stabilize again! Yet, there are differences between our recovery roller coaster and one you would find at an amusement part. You won't be approaching the ride from the top, which symbolizes a point free of pain. Instead, you are starting from a point partway down. Pain is already a factor. The first five stages of recovery will seem to take you the wrong way—deeper and deeper into pain. In our recovery model on page 94, the first steep drop will provide the impetus and the wherewithal for the uphill healing that comes later. Then you can look forward to more steady going. Just as the hills and valleys eventually level off in the roller-coaster ride, so also will your life. There will be other hills and valleys in your future, but none so extreme as what you are experiencing now. And you'll be equipped with the means to roll through them.

THE TEN STAGES OF THE RECOVERY CURVE

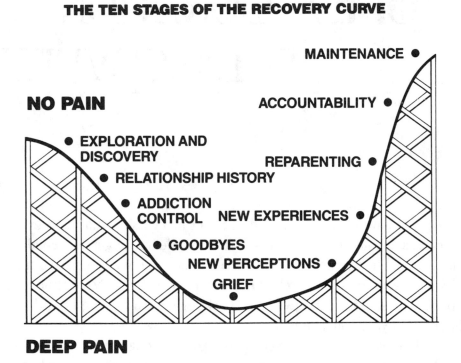

NO PAIN

MAINTENANCE ●

ACCOUNTABILITY ●

● EXPLORATION AND DISCOVERY

REPARENTING ●

● RELATIONSHIP HISTORY

● ADDICTION CONTROL   NEW EXPERIENCES ●

● GOODBYES

NEW PERCEPTIONS ●

GRIEF ●

DEEP PAIN

Before you begin this roller-coaster ride, you need to fasten your safety belt and make a firm commitment to the process ahead of you. How open have you been so far in the exploration process?

_____ I've surprised myself with all the things that are inside me.

_____ My feelings scare me, and I'm holding back.

_____ I'm being as open as I can.

Do you have any fears about going further in the healing process?
_____ yes _____ no

What are they? *(For instance, I'm worried that I'll never be free from all the pain inside me; I don't know if I have the strength to face all these issues.)*

_____

_____

_____

Are you willing to go deeper into your pain to the point of genuine grieving in order to break the destructive cycles of codependency in your life? _____ yes _____ no

What have you done so far that you are really proud of?
(For instance, I have faced the fact that my stepfather abused me. I have decided to forgive my mother for constantly criticizing me.)

_____

_____

_____

What do you want for your future? *(For instance, I want to stop repeating what happened to me and develop healthy relationships in my family.)*

_____

_____

_____

Stage One: Exploration and Discovery

This stage will not be completed by the end of this chapter. In fact, you've been working on this stage all during part one of this workbook, and you will continue to do so until you finish. The key to this stage is simply having the willingness to explore your life and discover clues about why you are the way you are.

We ask all patients to begin by making a short history of their lives. Write out significant facts and events that happened in each of the stages listed below. Include things like births, deaths, divorces, beginning school, moving, and hurts that you remember. Put at least three events in each category.

My life from birth to age four _____

_____

_____

_____

_____

My life from age five to age ten _____

_____

_____

_____

_____

My life from age eleven to age sixteen _____

_____

_____

_____

_____

_____

My life from age sixteen to age twenty _____

_____

_____

_____

_____

My life from age twenty until now _____

_____

_____

_____

_____

_____

_____

_____

_____

_____

This little catalog of events is meant to help you get an overview of your life, to see where you've been and where you are going. You will use and examine the information you have gathered here as we progress through the steps of the healing process.

Where Does God Fit In?

Codependency is really a problem of unhealthy relationships. If you want to heal your relationships, you must begin by healing yourself. God is waiting to play a significant part in your personal healing. He will give you the wisdom and strength to get you through the valleys and over the hills of your roller-coaster ride.

I think of God as

_____ a stern father waiting to catch me doing something wrong.
_____ an unconcerned entity who got the world rolling and then left it.
_____ a personal friend.
_____ loving for other people but not for me.
_____ someone who is just out of my reach.
_____ someone who betrayed me by letting all these horrible things happen to me.

The importance of taking time to discover who God is and how He wants to be involved in your life cannot be overemphasized. Finding God and entering into a relationship with Him are key factors in your recovery. Look at the benefits God promises those who trust in Him.

He will not forsake you.
Call upon Me in the day of trouble; I will deliver you, and you shall glorify Me. (Ps. 50:15)

He is always there for you.
The LORD is near to those who have a broken heart, and saves such as have a contrite spirit. (Ps. 34:18)

He is merciful when we fail.

Through the LORD'S mercies we are not consumed, because His compassions fail not. They are new every morning; great is Your faithfulness. (Lam. 3:22–23)

He has good plans for us.

'For I know the thoughts that I think toward you,' says the LORD, 'thoughts of peace and not of evil, to give you a future and a hope.' (Jer. 29:11)

He gives us power to become new.

Therefore, if anyone is in Christ, he is a new creation; old things have passed away; behold, all things have become new. (2 Cor. 5:17)

He adopts us as sons and daughters.

But when the fullness of the time had come, God sent forth His Son, born of a woman, born under law, to redeem those who were under the law, that we might receive the adoption as sons. (Gal. 4:4–5)

He gives us strength to change our codependency.

The LORD will give strength to His people; The LORD will bless His people with peace. (Ps. 29:11)

I have always felt a certain distance from God because *(for instance, I never thought He could accept me; I blamed Him for the bad things in my life)*

_____

_____,

but these verses have shown me that *(for instance, God does accept me, even with all my faults; God wants to heal me, not harm me)*

_____

_____

In my new relationship with God, I will concentrate on the fact that *(for instance, He loves me unconditionally and will never give up on me; He will give me the strength to cope with my situation)*

_____

_____

A New Focus

With God as your partner, you can approach the difficult relationships in your life with new hope and confidence. It's time now to narrow your field and single out the relationships you're going to work on as you go through the rest of this book.

Who am I currently in a codependent relationship with?
(For instance, my father, my husband, my boss, my best friend.)

1. _____

2. _____

3. _____

4. _____

5. _____

How am I codependent with each of these people? What unhealthy patterns have I developed? *(For instance, I'm always seeking my father's approval; I'm afraid to tell my husband what I think or believe; I'm taking responsibility for things my boss should be doing; I let my best friend use me.)*

1. _____

_____

2. _____

_____

3. _____

_____

4. _____

_____

5. _____

_____

In what ways has my codependent behavior been

A. self-destructive? *(For instance, I've become mute in my relationships, and I'm just trying to please other people. I'm feeling unhappy and depressed, but nobody seems to notice.)*

_____

_____

_____

_____

B. destructive to others? *(For instance, I'm letting other people use me, and they don't have to take responsibility for what they do—I'm always rescuing them.)*

_____

_____

_____

_____

_____

In what ways have I broken out of denial? *(For instance, I have acknowledged that the subtle abuses in my family were damaging to me.)*

_____

_____

_____

_____

I am willing to take the following steps to keep myself open to further exploration and new discoveries:

_____ I will validate what I've learned about myself by sharing it with someone else.

_____ I will join a support group.

_____ I will reread what I have written and validate it for myself.

THOUGHT CHECK

One thing that I've done that I can feel good about is _____

_____

_____

I need to follow up on _____

_____

An important new insight I've gained is that _____

9. RELATIONSHIP HISTORY/ INVENTORY, PART ONE

With the exception of the very few institutionalized, abandoned, or orphaned infants, nearly all of us are born into a nuclear family. We carry that primary family relationship with us, in one way or another, for our whole lives. We all maintain some sort of contact with our parents and siblings, even after their deaths. Since your parents and siblings played such a significant part in making you the person you are today, they will be our first focus in your relationship history and inventory.

In chapter 10 you will broaden your inventory to include significant relationships outside the family. Working through these chapters may be a time-consuming task, but it is absolutely essential to solving your codependency. You will uncover some very revealing patterns and trends that will help you understand how to improve the way you relate to yourself and to others. Later on in the healing process, you will be called upon to untangle each relationship, call to mind people both living and dead, and make peace with each one in an appropriate way.

This will involve bringing your relationships into clear and deliberate focus. You are not to pass judgment by assigning right or wrong or arbitrarily dismissing a memory as being irrelevant or too embarrassing to handle. For this exercise to be effective, you must be conscientious and thorough. Examining your significant relationships, both past and present, and coming to some resolution about them is essential to your healing.

A Brief Example

Peggy came to a Minirth-Meier Clinic for help after she became aware of her codependency at a seminar. She was distraught, trapped in a miserable marriage. At the beginning of her counseling, we asked her to do a brief survey of her relationships. The only connecting theme she could find was the obvious one: they were all unhealthy.

A more thorough relationship inventory brought some significant discoveries to light for Peggy. Although she was involved with a variety of very different individuals, a recurring theme ran through all the relationships. Pinpointing that theme became a key to changing her codependent behavior. Let's take a look at Peggy's inventory and at the trends she was able to identify.

Father—a workaholic. Peggy felt abandoned by him. She learned that the only way to get his attention was to perform. She learned from this relationship that it hurts to care about people, that having a relationship meant abandonment, winning love, and then getting hurt.

Opposite sex—she thought the men in her life were quite different. The most serious ones were Danny, a college sweetheart, and Robert, her husband. Danny and Robert were extremes. Danny was the opposite of her father—a free spirit, open with his emotions, and also an alcoholic and drug abuser. Peggy began to feel significant as a rescuer in his life. She thought, "If only I am good enough, I can pull him away from drugs." Of course, all her efforts were futile. She learned from that relationship that she would end up getting hurt, no matter what she did.

Authority figures—a special one was her eighth-grade science teacher, who became a mentor, tutor, and father substitute. However, he made a sexual pass at her, which ended the relationship. After that incident she felt extremely afraid and awkward around him. She received a confused message that if men are good to you, all they want is sex.

Present relationships—when Peggy married Robert, it was like marrying her father. He was a classic workaholic. In contrast to her college boyfriend, Danny, Robert was rigid and had high moral standards. His preoccupation with work left her feeling abandoned and worthless.

Looking briefly at these relationships, Peggy recognized these recurring themes:

- I always get lost or abandoned in relationships.
- I'm only worthwhile if I'm rescuing others or proving myself.
- Basically, I don't deserve to be happy in a relationship. I deserve to be hurt or punished.

Once Peggy knew that these basic beliefs were binding her to codependent behaviors, she could work on changing both the beliefs and the behaviors. She began by rewriting and correcting the beliefs so that changing the behaviors became much more natural.

We all have hidden themes, just as Peggy did, that work in our relationships on an unconscious level. They function like a built-in automatic radar system. Painful relationships and events that happen early in life become self-repeating and self-fulfilling prophecies. This radar is similar to a tracking system on a commercial aircraft—it sends out a signal and receives a signal. Codependents attract people and are attracted to people who fit the same negative codependent patterns.

This survey will help you to identify the repeating patterns in your adult life. When you recognize these patterns and bring them to a conscious awareness, you will be able to defuse the power of the radar system and reprogram it with healthy patterns.

SIBLINGS AND EXTENDED FAMILY

As you consider the dynamics at play within your family of origin (including siblings and members of your extended family), you will need to ask yourself this important question: **How was nurturance shared or distributed in my family?**

In counseling our clients, we often use the illustration of a large litter of puppies. Imagine, for a moment, what mealtime is like as these rambunctious, hungry puppies vie for positions near their mother and her milk. As the siblings line up to nurse, it's not unusual for the smallest—the runt of the litter—to be literally bumped to the end of the line. This smallest puppy is in danger of starving unless humans intervene and perhaps even hand-feed it until it is big enough to fend for itself.

Sometimes in families with three or more children the sheer number of people can result in an uneven distribution of nurturance. In smaller families, dysfunction within the family can create a similar environment.

How many people were there in your family during your growing-up years? _____

Were there others who, although not members of your family, played a significant role or consumed quantities of family time or attention?   ____ yes ____ no

Who were they? *(For instance, my mother babysat two other children, who were in our home several hours a week.)*

_____

_____

Once again, imagine that litter of puppies, all jockeying for position to receive nurturance from their mother. Now think of your family of origin. If you were to rank the members of your family in terms of how they fared at getting their needs met, where would you rank? *(For instance, first; last; in the middle.)*

_____

If you are an only child or came from a small family, your biggest competitors for nurturance might have been intangible things like careers or hobbies. What were the unseen competitors for your parents' time?

1. _____ work
2. _____ alcohol or drugs
3. _____ illness
4. _____ depression
5. _____ hobbies or interests
6. _____ climbing the social ladder
7. _____ caring for their aging parents

8. _____ (other) _____

In the following spaces, rank yourself with other members of your family in regard to getting the nurturance you needed. If you feel strongly that you were displaced by your parents' relationships with something other than siblings—something that you checked or filled in above—then feel free to include that in your ranking.

When it came to the distribution of attention in my family, my ranking in the family looked something like this:

1. _____

2. _____

3. _____

4. _____

5. _____

6. _____

I received more attention than did *(for instance, my older sister)*

_____

The person (or thing) who received more attention than I did was *(for instance, my father's car rebuilding project)*

_____

Overall, my needs for attention were:

_____ satisfied
_____ unsatisfied

When it came to the distribution of time in my family, my ranking in the family looked something like this:

1. _____

2. _____

3. _____

4. _____

5. _____

6. _____

I received more time than did _____

The person (or thing) who received more time than I did was

_____

Overall, my needs for time were:

_____ satisfied
_____ unsatisfied

When it came to the distribution of material resources in my family, my ranking in the family looked something like this:

1. _____

2. _____

3. _____

4. _____

5. _____

6. _____

I had access to more material resources than did _____

_____

The person (or thing) who received more material resources than I

did was _____

Overall, my needs for material things were:

_____ satisfied
_____ unsatisfied

Did you consistently rank near the top or bottom of your lists?

_____ top
_____ middle
_____ bottom

If you perceived a bottom ranking a good part of the time, your lack of nurturance may be fueling your codependency. On the other hand, if you consistently ranked first, you may have grown up realizing that siblings, or maybe even a parent, were not being treated fairly. This could have created a tremendous sense of guilt within you, which contributes to your codependency.

How do you feel about the way you ranked in your lists?
(For instance, I feel sad and left out; I feel fairly content.)

_____

_____

SIGNIFICANT EVENTS IN MY FAMILY OF ORIGIN

Early childhood events teach us how to relate to the world. Therefore, it is essential to recall specific memories from childhood to understand the underworkings of codependency in your life. Write one pleasurable memory and one painful memory that you associate with each person in your family of origin. Be specific and make sure you include any abuses—passive or active—that occurred.

Parents and siblings are specified in this survey, but be sure to write in names of other people who lived with or associated closely with your family of origin, such as live-in grandparents.

Father
Pleasurable: _____

_____

Painful: _____

_____

Mother
Pleasurable: _____

_____

Painful: _____

_____

Sibling (name) _____

Pleasurable: _____

_____

Painful: _____

_____

Sibling (name) _____

Pleasurable: _____

_____

Painful: _____

_____

Sibling (name) _____

Pleasurable: _____

_____

Painful: _____

_____

Stepparent/Grandparent (name) _____

Pleasurable: _____

_____

Painful: _____

_____

Stepparent/Grandparent (name) _____

Pleasurable: _____

_____

Painful: _____

_____

(If you have more family members than this space provides for, complete this part of the survey on an extra sheet of paper.)

SUMMARY

From looking over these experiences, what do you find is the most significant influence each family member had on you?

My mother's influence on me today can be seen in *(for instance, I turned out just like she was—I'm depressed and codependent with my own children)*

_____

_____

_____

_____

My father's influence on me today can be seen in *(for instance, his anger frightened me and I never wanted to be like him, so I don't get mad; I'm afraid to trust anyone because I couldn't trust him)*

_____

_____

_____

My siblings' influence on me today can be seen in *(for instance, I was always in competition with my sisters and feel very competitive in my relationships today)*

_____

_____

_____

_____

My grandparents' influence on me today can be seen in *(for instance, they were the most stabilizing factor in my life)*

_____

_____

_____

_____

The Effects of Codependency on Family Roles

Consider the many intricately woven interpersonal relationships in our lives: husband/wife, parent/child, boss/subordinate, sister/brother, clergy/layperson, teacher/student, to name just a few. One person usually plays several of these roles simultaneously. Add to this complicated set-up the issue of birth order: eldest, youngest, older brother/younger brother, older sister/younger sister. The person whose love tank is low unconsciously shifts these complex roles around, seeking to re-create the original family dynamic, hoping to get rid of the original family pain. The unconscious hope is that this time around the problem will be mended, the pain eased, the situation corrected.

Psychologists have also come to recognize that there are certain roles or stereotypes that people assume within a family. All families develop them to a certain extent—the hero, the scapegoat, the lost child, the mascot, and the enabler. For people in a dysfunctional family, these roles become a coping mechanism, a way to get through life with a minimum of upset. They become rigid, mindless patterns of behavior easily visible to those outside the family, yet unrecognized by those within. Check off the statements that apply to your growing-up years.

Hero

_____ I was a very responsible child.

_____ I took up the slack for my mom and dad with the other children in the family.

_____ I am very driven—to make straight A's, to achieve in my work, to keep everyone happy.

_____ I received a great deal of praise from teachers and pastors, which kept my love tank filled when my parents failed.

These responses are typical of the family hero, who is usually the oldest child, but not always. The hero often does not receive praise from the family about the things he or she does. But the hero's responsible personality is rewarded in social and school environments. The hero usually takes on the parent and adult responsibilities in the home at a very early age, doing the shopping, cleaning, and child care.

Scapegoat

_____ My parents often blamed me for the problems in our family.

_____ Many times my problems were the center of attention while my parents' dysfunctional problems were ignored.

_____ Most of my family members saw me as the source of their pain.

_____ I received the most negative attention in my family.

A scapegoat receives negative attention for rebellious and negative behavior. This negative attention just reinforces the undesirable behavior. Scapegoats are usually blamed for all the family problems, although there are usually obvious problems between the parents as well.

Mascot

_____ I didn't let my family problems get to me—I usually laughed them away.

_____ As long as I could make a joke, I knew my family would be okay after all.

_____ I'm good at forgetting the pain from my childhood.

_____ I was considered the baby of the family, and it was assumed that I would never "grow up."

A mascot earns attention by grabbing it. This person dissolves problems and pain with a joke. The mascot finds that the best way to deal with the dysfunctional family is to distract everyone from the distressing issues.

Lost Child

_____ I caused hardly any problems in my family.

_____ I always preferred to be by myself.

_____ My parents have said of me, ". . . was never a problem."

_____ I liked playing or reading alone.

The lost child is usually unnoticed. This person prefers to be alone and escapes the pain of the dysfunctional family by trying to get along and staying out of everyone's way. The lost child is nice—constantly, unbearably, doggedly nice.

From the list above, choose the roles you played in your family of origin.

In my family I was the _____ most of the

time. I was the _____ some of the time.

I was never the _____

THE ROLES MY FAMILY PLAYED

Write the names of the family members who played each of these roles in your family of origin.

Hero _____

Scapegoat _____

Mascot _____

Lost Child _____

Every person in a dysfunctional family is an enabler who contributes to the family dysfunction in a particular way. Every family has a mascot, a lost child, a hero, and a scapegoat to some degree. The role of enabler is a deeper layer behind each of the roles. The following are examples of ways you may have been an enabler. Check the statements that apply to you.

Placater

_____ I always tried to make it all better somehow.
_____ I was the one in the family who had a knack for saying the right words to smooth things out.

The placater is the smooth talker who tries to keep the family friction at a minimum.

Martyr

_____ I would do anything to make things work out for my family.
_____ I usually ended up losing out on things I wanted in order to alleviate a tense family situation.

As the word implies, the martyr sacrifices time, energy, and happiness to keep the family together. The martyr's needs are never considered as legitimate in his or her own eyes as the needs of others in the family.

Rescuer

_____ I was the one in my family who tried to solve the problems.
_____ When I see a problem, I want to fix it as soon as possible.

The rescuer is different from the martyr in that the resolution of family problems doesn't involve self-sacrifice. The rescuer just wants to get things resolved as soon as possible and then get on with life.

Persecutor

_____ I've known what was wrong with my family since I was a child.
_____ People get irritated with me because I call them on the issues.

The persecutor is always fixing the blame on someone. A barely controlled undercurrent of rage and anger makes this person difficult to be around.

Victim

_____ Bad things just happen to me.
_____ No one who endured my childhood could grow up to be a happy person.

The victim is the self-pitier who feels that all chances at happiness have been destroyed because of unfortunate and unfair circumstances in childhood.

In which way were you an enabler in your family of origin?
(*Circle one.*)

Placater   Martyr   Rescuer   Persecutor   Victim

In which way are you an enabler in your present relationships?
(Circle one.)

Placater   Martyr   Rescuer   Persecutor   Victim

Placater, martyr, rescuer, persecutor, victim, hero, scapegoat, mascot, lost child—family members learn these roles well. But the roles are warped. The later stages of recovery will teach you how to live beyond these roles. Just being able to recognize which parts you played is an important step in recovering from codependency.

Relationships with Family Members and Friends

In a relationship history and inventory it is helpful to consider relationships in every area of your life as you work through your life chronologically. Don't tell yourself the relationship was not important—try to fill in the blanks completely. You have already considered the relationships in your family of origin. Now consider other relationships that were significant to you (other relatives, friends, mentors, confidantes, rivals). You'll be examining how each relationship changed you and whether you may have inflicted hurt or experienced hurt through your interaction with these significant people in your life.

CHILDHOOD RELATIONSHIPS

One significant relationship from my childhood years was
(for instance, kindergarten teacher)

_____

My memories of this person include _____

_____

_____

_____

This person hurt me by _____

_____

I hurt this person when I _____

_____

_____

I would describe the current status of this relationship as _____

_____

_____

If the relationship is "over," how did it end? _____

_____

Summing up the relationship in a single phrase, I would say that

_____

_____

One significant relationship from my childhood years was _____

_____

My memories of this person include _____

_____

_____

_____

This person hurt me by _____

_____

I hurt this person when I _____

_____

_____

I would describe the current status of this relationship as _____

_____

_____

If the relationship is "over," how did it end? _____

_____

Summing up the relationship in a single phrase, I would say that

_____

_____

One significant relationship from my childhood years was _____

_____

My memories of this person include _____

_____

_____

_____

This person hurt me by _____

_____

I hurt this person when I _____

_____

_____

I would describe the current status of this relationship as _____

_____

_____

If the relationship is "over," how did it end? _____

_____

Summing up the relationship in a single phrase, I would say that

_____

_____

TEENAGE RELATIONSHIPS

One significant relationship from my teenage years was *(for instance, track coach)*

_____

My memories of this person include _____

_____

_____

_____

This person hurt me by _____

_____

I hurt this person when I _____

_____

_____

I would describe the current status of this relationship as _____

_____

_____

If the relationship is "over," how did it end? _____

_____

Summing up the relationship in a single phrase, I would say that

_____

_____

One significant relationship from my teenage years was _____

_____

My memories of this person include _____

_____

_____

_____

This person hurt me by _____

I hurt this person when I _____

I would describe the current status of this relationship as _____

If the relationship is "over," how did it end? _____

Summing up the relationship in a single phrase, I would say that

One significant relationship from my teenage years was _____

My memories of this person include _____

This person hurt me by _____

I hurt this person when I _____ _____

_____

_____

I would describe the current status of this relationship as _____

_____

_____

If the relationship is "over," how did it end? _____

_____

Summing up the relationship in a single phrase, I would say that

_____

_____

EARLY-ADULT RELATIONSHIPS

One significant relationship from my early-adult years was
(for instance, first boss)

_____

My memories of this person include _____

_____

_____

_____

This person hurt me by _____

_____

I hurt this person when I _____

_____

_____

I would describe the current status of this relationship as _____

_____

_____

If the relationship is "over," how did it end? _____

_____

Summing up the relationship in a single phrase, I would say that

_____

_____

One significant relationship from my early-adult years was _____

_____

My memories of this person include _____

_____

_____

_____

This person hurt me by _____

_____

I hurt this person when I _____

_____

_____

I would describe the current status of this relationship as _____

_____

_____

If the relationship is "over," how did it end? _____

_____

Summing up the relationship in a single phrase, I would say that

_____

_____

One significant relationship from my early-adult years was _____

_____

My memories of this person include _____

_____

_____

_____

This person hurt me by _____

_____

I hurt this person when I _____

_____

_____

I would describe the current status of this relationship as _____

_____

_____

If the relationship is "over," how did it end? _____

_____

Summing up the relationship in a single phrase, I would say that

_____

_____

PRESENT RELATIONSHIPS

One significant relationship from the present is *(for instance, best friend)*

_____

My memories of this person include _____

_____

_____

_____

This person hurt me by _____

_____

I hurt this person when I _____

_____

_____

I would describe the current status of this relationship as _____

_____

_____

If the relationship is "over," how did it end? _____

_____

Summing up the relationship in a single phrase, I would say that

_____

_____

One significant relationship from the present is _____

_____

My memories of this person include _____

_____

_____

_____

This person hurt me by _____

_____

I hurt this person when I _____

_____

_____

I would describe the current status of this relationship as _____

_____

_____

If the relationship is "over," how did it end? _____

_____

Summing up the relationship in a single phrase, I would say that

_____

_____

One significant relationship from the present is _____

_____

My memories of this person include _____

_____

_____

_____

This person hurt me by _____

_____

I hurt this person when I _____

_____

I would describe the current status of this relationship as _____

_____

If the relationship is "over," how did it end? _____

_____

Summing up the relationship in a single phrase, I would say that

_____

_____

Summary

A lot of my relationships seem similar in that *(for instance, either I'm a victim or I'm rescuing people)*

_____

_____

A mistake in relationships that I've made more than once is *(for instance, I'm not a good judge of character—I can't choose the right person to trust)*

_____

_____

_____

I'm not sure why, but I always seem to get hurt because
(for instance, I let people take advantage of me)

_____

_____

_____

From my Relationship Inventory, I can identify these unconscious patterns in my adult life. *(For instance, I always feel the need to prove myself; I always end up being used by people; I can't really trust or feel close to anybody.)*

1. _____

_____

2. _____

_____

3. _____

_____

Good work! In the next chapter the hidden themes in your relationships will continue to unfold as you broaden the scope of your relationship inventory.

10. RELATIONSHIP HISTORY/ INVENTORY, PART TWO

Codependency patterns are not limited to your family; they have influenced every significant relationship in your life. In this chapter we're going to ask you to expand your relationship history and inventory to include others with whom you've been emotionally involved. First, you will review your relationships with members of the opposite sex and with authority figures. Then you will search for themes in the ways you relate to yourself, people of the same sex, and professional caregivers. Finally, you will take an inventory of your relationship with God. Each of these areas will bring out important issues that will promote your healing from codependency.

Relationships with the Opposite Sex

Take a moment to reflect on your significant relationships with the opposite sex. Who are the significant people you dated, you wanted to date, or were your close friends? List and evaluate those relationships.

1. *(name)* _____

   What attracted you: _____

   How you were hurt: _____

   What you learned about yourself/opposite sex: _____

   _____

2. *(name)* _____

   What attracted you: _____

   How you were hurt: _____

   What you learned about yourself/opposite sex: _____

   _____

3. *(name)* _____

   What attracted you: _____

   How you were hurt: _____

   What you learned about yourself/opposite sex: _____

   _____

4. *(name)* _____

   What attracted you: _____

   How you were hurt: _____

   What you learned about yourself/opposite sex: _____

   _____

5. *(name)* _____

What attracted you: _____

How you were hurt: _____

What you learned about yourself/opposite sex: _____

_____

6. *(name)* _____

What attracted you: _____

How you were hurt: _____

What you learned about yourself/opposite sex: _____

_____

7. *(name)* _____

What attracted you: _____

How you were hurt: _____

What you learned about yourself/opposite sex: _____

_____

8. *(name)* _____

What attracted you: _____

How you were hurt: _____

What you learned about yourself/opposite sex: _____

_____

Do you see any patterns in these relationships?
_____ yes _____ no

How would you characterize your relationship with your opposite-sex parent? *(For instance, I felt very comfortable and accepted; I felt unwanted and pushed aside.)*

_____

_____

_____

How did your relationship with your opposite-sex parent influence your other relationships with the opposite sex? *(For instance, I felt rejected by my father, and so I've always needed a lot of male attention; I felt controlled by my mother, and I let women control me.)*

_____

_____

_____

SUMMARY

What have you learned about yourself in general through your relationships with the opposite sex? *(For instance, that I get hurt a lot, that I desperately need to have a boyfriend/girlfriend to feel good about myself.)*

_____

_____

_____

Authority Figures

Your relationships with authority figures, both past and present, can shape the way you seek, accept, and wield power. Think over the authority figures you have dealt with—they might include your parents, pastor, babysitter, teacher, coach, boss, mentor, or grandparent—anyone who has had a significant level of control over your life. Choose four of them for this exercise and write one name on the first line of each of the four sections below. Once you have written in the four names, go back and answer the remaining questions in each section.

(name 1) _____

How did this person treat you? _____

_____

How did you respond to his or her authority—did you follow

blindly or did you rebel in any way? _____

_____

What leadership techniques did this person use to which you

responded well? _____

_____

Describe any way this person abused his or her power. _____

_____

_____

Check the words that show how you felt about yourself when you were under this person's authority. _____ good _____ bad _____ content _____ oppressed _____ powerless _____ productive

What were your feelings toward this person when you were under his or her authority? _____

_____

Was he or she fair? _____ yes _____ no

If not, why not? _____

_____

Looking back, do you wish you had responded differently to this person's leadership or use of power? _____ yes _____ no

How? _____

_____

How did your time under this person's authority shape your view of power? _____

_____

(name 2) _____

How did this person treat you? _____

_____

How did you respond to his or her authority—did you follow blindly or did you rebel in any way? _____

_____

What leadership techniques did this person use to which you responded well? _____

_____

Describe any way this person abused his or her power. _____

_____

_____

Check the words that show how you felt about yourself when you were under this person's authority. _____ good _____ bad _____ content _____ oppressed _____ powerless _____ productive

What were your feelings toward this person when you were under

his or her authority? _____

_____

Was he or she fair? _____ yes _____ no

If not, why not? _____

_____

Looking back, do you wish you had responded differently to this person's leadership or use of power? _____ yes _____ no

How? _____

_____

How did your time under this person's authority shape your view of

power? _____

_____

(name 3) _____

How did this person treat you? _____

_____

How did you respond to his or her authority—did you follow

blindly or did you rebel in any way? _____

_____

What leadership techniques did this person use to which you

responded well? _____

_____

Describe any way this person abused his or her power. _____

_____

_____

Check the words that show how you felt about yourself when you
were under this person's authority. _____ good _____ bad
_____ content _____ oppressed _____ powerless _____ productive

What were your feelings toward this person when you were under

his or her authority? _____

_____

Was he or she fair? _____ yes _____ no

If not, why not? _____

_____

Looking back, do you wish you had responded differently to this person's leadership or use of power?   _____ yes _____ no

How? _____

_____

How did your time under this person's authority shape your view of

power? _____

_____

(name 4) _____

How did this person treat you? _____

_____

How did you respond to his or her authority—did you follow

blindly or did you rebel in any way? _____

_____

What leadership techniques did this person use to which you

responded well? _____

_____

Describe any way this person abused his or her power. _____

_____

_____

Check the words that show how you felt about yourself when you were under this person's authority.   _____ good _____ bad
_____ content _____ oppressed _____ powerless _____ productive

What were your feelings toward this person when you were under his or her authority? _____

_____

Was he or she fair?   ____ yes ____ no

If not, why not? _____

_____

Looking back, do you wish you had responded differently to this person's leadership or use of power?   ____ yes ____ no

How? _____

_____

How did your time under this person's authority shape your view of power? _____

_____

SUMMARY

From the authority figures in my life, I learned to *(circle one)*

accept   fear   dislike   despise   respect

authority.

Looking back over the preceding inventory, do you see any patterns in your relationships with authority? *(For instance, I related better to men in authority than to women.)*

_____

_____

_____

Have you been exposed to a series of authority figures who used their power in an abusive or destructive manner?
_____ yes _____ no

Have you had healthy models of authority from which to pattern your own perspective of power?   _____ yes _____ no

How could your relationship to authority figures be affecting your codependency? *(For instance, I've always felt so controlled by other people that now I am very controlling of others. My self-esteem is very low, and I always expect to be criticized by my superiors.)*

_____

_____

_____

Relationship with Yourself

Perhaps you have never considered the fact that you actually have a relationship with yourself. But you do—and it's important. Part of healing from codependency involves coming to terms with your self-esteem, the negative messages you perpetuate, and finally making peace with yourself. Begin by listing the things you don't like about yourself.

I don't like me because _____

_____

_____

_____

_____

_____

_____

_____

_____

This next step is a little more difficult, but absolutely necessary. You are to write a letter introducing yourself. If you have trouble completing it, ask a supportive friend for suggestions. Write the letter to an imaginary new friend, saying only positive things about yourself. Do not criticize yourself in any way.

Dear _____,

_____

_____

_____

_____

_____

_____

_____

_____

Same-Sex Relationships

Our identity and self-image is very much influenced by how we accept being the gender that we are. Donna was the second daughter of a man who wanted only two children, but deeply wanted a son. Donna became the classic tomboy, while her older sister, Elizabeth, was the very epitome of femininity. Donna saw her gender as the one thing that kept her from having what she wanted. She enjoyed more of her father's attention than her sister did, but she never felt quite fulfilled. In her survey Donna found a deep hate for women—she saw them as weak and vulnerable.

When Donna finally came to terms with the fact that she hated women because she was weak and vulnerable herself, she found a reason to break away from her codependent relationships that involved rescuing other women. Admitting to a universal vulnerability helped her to grow closer to her boyfriend. Her relationship with her father had led her to believe that men would love her only if she was strong and self-sufficient. The truth was that her boyfriend was glad to know that she had needs, and he wanted to share his own needs with her as well.

Beginning with your parents, inventory the significant relationships with your gender and think about how these relationships influenced your life.

My mother's views about my gender were *(for instance, my mother thought all men were abusive, and so she hated me)*

_____

_____

_____

_____

My father's views about my gender were *(for instance, he thought women were inferior to men, and I had less status in the family than my brothers)*

_____

_____

_____

_____

For this part of the survey, choose five people of your gender with whom you shared significant relationships, past or present. The list may include your best friend, school or work mates, and siblings.

(name 1) _____

What I learned about my gender: _____

_____

_____

(name 2) _____

What I learned about my gender: _____

_____

_____

(name 3) _____

What I learned about my gender: _____

_____

_____

(name 4) _____

What I learned about my gender: _____

_____

_____

(name 5) _____

What I learned about my gender: _____

_____

_____

SUMMARY

For me, being a woman/man *(circle one)* means *(for instance, I'm not as important as people of the other sex; I've got a lot to prove)*

_____

_____

_____

_____

_____

_____

Relationships with Professional Care-Givers

In your lifetime you have encountered various care-givers, including pastors and people in health- and mental health-care fields. These people hold an important place in society. We naturally assume that we can trust them to have our best interests at heart. Think about how you have related to professional care-givers.

Did you ever feel that a professional care-giver used power and influence inappropriately? _____ yes _____ no

Write the names of significant care-givers in your life. Then write how you feel about the treatment you received from those individuals.

(name 1) _____

I feel that this person *(for example, my orthodontist made me feel uncomfortable because he said sexually suggestive things to me)*

_____

_____

I responded by *(for instance, being very guarded in his presence)*

_____

_____

(name 2) _____

I feel that this person _____

_____

_____

I responded by _____

_____

_____

(name 3) _____

I feel that this person _____

_____

_____

I responded by _____

_____

_____

(name 4) _____

I feel that this person _____

_____

_____

I responded by _____

_____

_____

(name 5) _____

I feel that this person _____

_____

_____

I responded by _____

_____

_____

What did you learn from these significant relationships about being able to put trust in your care-giver? *(For instance, I really felt as if I was important and they cared about the concerns I brought; I knew I had to trust them, but I felt tense about it.)*

_____

_____

What did you learn about yourself from the treatment you received from these professionals? *(For instance, that I was important to somebody; that everyone takes advantage of me.)*

_____

_____

Relationship with God

How does a codependent relationship with God differ from a healthy one? Think of it in the terms you have been exploring so far. Gladys grew up with a father who could not or would not listen to her. She unconsciously attributed that trait to her husband, John, as well, despite his willingness to listen. If she unconsciously attributes that same human imperfection to God, her power of prayer will be severely hampered. She will be unable to appreciate God's loving nature, so she may well agree with those who say an intimate relationship with God is unattainable. In her case she will be right. Intimacy with God will evade her, not because of God's nature, but because of that codependent blinder she's wearing.

Do you set humanistic limits on God?   ____ yes ____ no

Have you unconsciously attributed some of your father's negative personality traits to God?   ____ yes ____ no

Which ones? *(For instance, my dad was a rageaholic, and I see God as wrathful.)*

_____

_____

When I think back to my growing up years, I would describe the relationship my parents had with God as *(for instance, they talked about God, but their lives weren't consistent with what they said)*

_____

_____

Sometimes when we look back on the disappointing or even tragic moments of our lives, we experience the natural urge to place blame—to resolve the unhappiness by identifying the source. Yet, there are times when identifying the true origin of the crisis can create even greater pain. For example, recognizing yourself as the source of a painful mistake, or a parent as the source of emotional abandonment, or a respected relative as the source of sexual abuse can generate additional pain. It's tempting to find an unseen and less threatening third party to bear the blame. As a result, God sometimes becomes the scapegoat for choices that are actually made by people.

Go back to the hurts or crises for which you've been blaming God.

Is there another person who is more directly responsible for any of those disappointments? _____ yes _____ no

I admit that I've been bitter toward God regarding *(for instance, the fact that my mom was an alcoholic)*

_____ ;

yet, the person directly responsible for that event was *(for instance, my mother)*

_____

I admit that I've been bitter toward God regarding _____

_____ ;

yet, the person directly responsible for that event was _____

_____

I admit that I've been bitter toward God regarding _____

_____ ;

yet, the person directly responsible for that event was _____

_____

I admit that I've been bitter toward God regarding _____

_____ ;

yet, the person directly responsible for that event was _____

_____

Jesus used the concept of a strong family under a loving, nurturing father when He said, "What man is there among you who, if his son asks for bread, will give him a stone? Or if he asks for a fish, will he give him a serpent? If you then, being evil, know how to give good gifts to your children, how much more will your Father who is in heaven give good things to those who ask Him!" (Matt. 7:9–11). The earthly family becomes the shadow of the heavenly family, with God as the all-wise, all-nurturing head. A solid, nurturing, stable family is the core of God's plan for our happiness, long life, and a clear understanding of His love for us.

No human can completely comprehend who God is. But when we look at the whole of Scripture, there emerges a multidimensional picture of a wonderful Master whose love for us is incomprehensible. Even as He demands, He understands. He loves faultlessly, guides perfectly, and reigns absolutely. But any relationship is a two-way street. God will not barge into your life—He awaits your invitation.

I've tried to draw close to God by *(for instance, going to church; taking part in a Bible study)*

_____

_____

Something I might consider doing to help me feel closer to God is *(for instance, taking time to pray and listen to Him daily)*

_____

_____

Summary

You've assembled a lot of information in these two chapters. Now it's time to look back at the conclusions you drew in each section and record them here.

I discovered the following patterns in my relationship with

MY FAMILY *(For instance, I never felt wanted or accepted; my needs were unfulfilled.)*

_____

_____

_____

MY FRIENDS *(For instance, I always seem to choose the wrong kind of people, and I end up being used.)*

_____

_____

_____

OPPOSITE SEX *(For instance, I feel unattractive and ill at ease with the opposite sex.)*

_____

_____

_____

AUTHORITY *(For instance, it's difficult for me to trust anyone in authority.)*

_____

_____

_____

SAME SEX *(For instance, many of my same-sex relationships have involved jealousy and mistrust.)*

_____

_____

_____

SELF *(For instance, I found that there are a lot of things I don't like about myself.)*

_____

_____

_____

PROFESSIONAL CARE-GIVERS *(For instance, it's been difficult for me to receive care.)*

_____

_____

_____

GOD *(For instance, I attributed a lot of my father's negative characteristics to God.)*

_____

_____

_____

My unconscious radar system has been sending out these messages *(for instance, I don't deserve to be happy, so go ahead and hurt me; if I trust people I'll always get hurt, so keep your distance; the only way I can be happy is if I control the lives of people who are important to me, so let me control you):*

_____

_____

_____

_____

_____

_____

You've come to some new insights and drawn some important new conclusions about yourself. At this point it would be very beneficial to share these insights with a mature, trusted friend. Remember, you're walking away from unhealthy relationships and toward healthier ones. Sharing your journey is important. A friend will be able to validate what you've learned and offer new insights as well.

The next chapter will help you to identify and break away from the addictive factors in your life.

11. ADDICTION CONTROL

Ever since George was a young boy, he has felt tremendously responsible for his mother's welfare. While his workaholic father was preoccupied and out of the house, George tried to meet his mother's emotional needs. As an adult, George lives just a few miles from his old home. As his mother has gotten older, she's come to depend on him more and more. George resents her constant demands for help and the way she intrudes on his time, especially because of the tension it creates with his wife and family. But he feels compelled to meet his mother's every need. Each time she calls, he's at her side within minutes. George's codependent relationship with his mother is both addictive and destructive.

When counselors first began to deal with the issue of codependency, they assumed it was strictly an effect—a syndrome found in people who lived with alcoholics or other addicts. But now we understand that codependency is also a cause—an original source of pain which traps people in its own vicious cycles of addiction. Much of this workbook has been devoted to helping you discover the sources of your codependency—but identifying your pain is not enough. Now it's time to take definite steps to recover from both the codependency and the additive cycle that feeds it.

Our model of the addiction cycle looks like a spiraling circle. It begins with pain of some sort—guilt, low self-esteem, dissatisfaction, pressure, or even boredom. To ease the pain, the subject turns to some kind of anesthetic, like alcohol, drugs, an illicit sexual encounter, a shopping binge, or a gambling spree. The consequences of using this anesthetic are remorse, more guilt, and even more pain. The cycle goes around again as the subject returns to the anesthetic of choice. The consequences of this addictive behavior can increase to include depression, loss of health, and in some cases, the loss of job and family. More guilt and shame, more remorse, more anesthetic. The cure has now turned into the cause, and the cycle is rolling on its own completely apart from the initial pain.

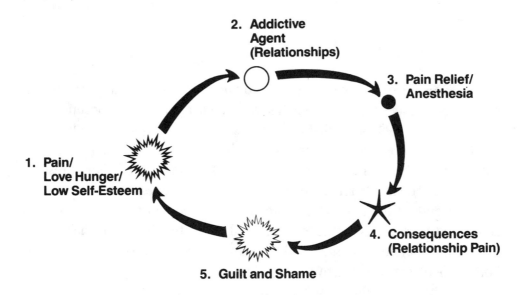

For a codependent person, the cycle works in exactly the same way; however, the addictive agent is not drugs or alcohol—it is unhealthy relationships. In George's case the love hunger resulted from a lack of nurturance from his workaholic father and codependent mother. Now, added to that pain is the additional hurt of feeling distanced and alienated from his wife. George's addictive agent is his relationship with his mother. His anesthesia is the feeling of significance and adequacy that comes when he helps her out and protects her. George suffers the consequences of an irate family who feel deserted and displaced. As his wife and children grow more and more distant, George feels guilty and ashamed that he can't meet everyone's needs and keep his family happy. He feels helpless, torn in his loyalties, and out of control. George's feelings of inadequacy compound his original pain; he goes to the only anesthetic he knows—helping his mother—and the cycle spirals downward. George knows his behavior with his mother is not normal, but he doesn't know how to break away from it.

Your Addiction Cycle

This chapter is devoted to helping you identify the addictive agents in your life and develop a strategy for breaking the vicious cycle that is pulling you down. We will work through the addiction cycle step-by-step.

1. PAIN/LOVE HUNGER/LOW SELF-ESTEEM

As you completed the Relationship History/Inventory in the previous two chapters, you identified many painful events and relationships from early childhood years to the present. These may have included rejection by a parent, abuse, death of a loved one, a disastrous love affair, trauma at work, or an encounter with a disfiguring or debilitating disease.

> Which of these issues stands out in your mind as being central to the love hunger and low self-esteem that you're experiencing now? Try to identify four pain factors in your life. *(For instance, my wife makes me feel like dirt. I never feel confident of my ability to do anything. My father has always made me feel like I'm not quite good enough. My husband is an alcoholic, and our life is a mess.)*

1. _____

_____

2. _____

_____

3. _____

_____

4. _____

_____

2. ADDICTIVE AGENTS

An alcoholic's addictive agent is easy to identify—it comes in a bottle. For the codependent, discovering the addictive agent may require a bit of detective work. Read through this list of possible addictive agents and check the ones that apply to you.

Martyrdom

_____ If I don't take care of him/her, he/she will fall apart.
_____ I'm supposed to put others first.

Denial

_____ His/her problems aren't really that bad.
_____ I'm just helping him/her out during a hard time.

Rescuing

_____ After all, I like helping other people.
_____ If I don't help, who will?

Work

_____ I bring at least an hour's worth of work home three or more
nights a week.

_____ Work must come first—it's our livelihood, after all.

Spending

_____ I have had to ask for a raise on my credit limit because of my spending habits.
_____ Paying my monthly bills is always touch-and-go.

Sexual Activities

_____ I read or look at pornographic material.
_____ I spend a lot of time thinking about sex.

Relationship

_____ I call *(name)* _____ at least twice daily.
_____ When I don't hear from *(name)* _____ I feel anxiety.

Rage

_____ I feel much better when I blow up at somebody.
_____ I've just got to vent my anger at someone or I'll explode.

Devotion to an Organization or Cause

_____ I would feel guilty if I stopped supporting *(name one of your causes)* _____
_____ I would be a bad person if I spent less of my time and resources on *(name an organization)* _____

Television

_____ I watch three or more hours of television a day.
_____ When I feel anxious, angry, or hurt I turn on the T.V.

Computer Games and Programs

_____ I spend nearly all my leisure time playing computer games.

_____ I neglect some important responsibilities because I am playing computer games and programs.

Hobbies

_____ My hobby *(golf, exercise, crafts)* keeps me from taking care of my responsibilities.

_____ I live to do my hobby.

Alcohol/Drugs

_____ I use alcohol/drugs to cover up my pain.

_____ I like my personality better when I'm using drugs or alcohol.

Hypochondria

_____ When something bothers me I usually end up sick in bed.

_____ I have physical problems *(aches and pains)* that the doctors can't seem to identify.

Legalism

_____ I feel comfortable living by the letter of the law.

_____ My relationships are suffering because I am so concerned about doctrine.

Food

_____ I use food as an anesthesia for pain.

_____ When I feel bad, I eat.

As you can see, your addictive agent can go beyond relationships. List all the nonrelationship addictive agents you checked above. Also list any others that have come to mind as you've done this exercise.

My addictive agents include:

1. _____

2. _____

3. _____

4. _____

Now think about your addictive relationships.

Do you feel the need to monopolize and control someone?
_____ yes _____ no

(name) _____

Do you anxiously maintain constant contact with someone?
_____ yes _____ no

(name) _____

Do you tend to draw your self-esteem from one individual?
_____ yes _____ no

(name) _____

Do you feel that someone is smothering you, but you're afraid to try to escape?   _____ yes _____ no

(name) _____

Do you feel particularly responsible for everything that happens to a specific person?   _____ yes _____ no

(name) _____

Besides the people listed here, are there others with whom you share an addictive relationship?   _____ yes _____ no

List their names here.

1. _____

2. _____

3. _____

3. PAIN RELIEF/ANESTHESIA

For each of the nonrelationship addictions you listed, tell how involvement with that addictive agent makes you feel. *(For instance, buying new clothes makes me feel pretty and important. Doing volunteer work makes me feel worthwhile. I get so lost in my hobby I don't even realize I'm unhappy. The world on TV takes me away from my unhappiness.)*

1. _____

_____

2. _____

_____

3. _____

_____

4. _____

_____

Tell what sort of anesthesia you get from each of the relationships you listed above. *(For instance, I feel needed; I feel alive and worthwhile. We get lost in each other's problems. I feel content and relaxed to have him in my control.)*

1. _____

_____

2. _____

_____

3. _____

_____

4. _____

_____

4. CONSEQUENCES

Consequences are a powerful dynamic. As you face the consequences of your addictions, you may find yourself pulled rapidly to a new depth within the addictive cycle.

Consequences are the "effects" related to the "cause" of your compulsions. Their power is derived from the guilt and shame that accompanies them. The consequences that hold the most power over you are the negative ones, even though there can be some positive elements that drive your addiction. Take, for instance, the perfectionistic housekeeper. One consequence of this addiction is a spotless house. Yet, even though she reaps the compliments of friends and family who praise her housekeeping, their remarks may contrast painfully with how trapped and out of control she feels on the inside.

Identify the consequences, both positive and negative, of the addictions you have listed in this chapter.

Benefit: *(My workaholism resulted in more money for my family.)*
Consequence: *(Every time money rolled in, I thought of my kids, who were paying the price for my absence, and I cringed.)*

Benefit: _____

_____

Consequence: _____

_____

Benefit: _____

_____

Consequence: _____

_____

Benefit: _____

_____

Consequence: _____

_____

Benefit: _____

_____

Consequence: _____

_____

A consequence can color every area of your life. It affects you physically, emotionally, financially, socially, and spiritually. Work through the consequences of each of the addictions you identified above.

Addiction #1: _____

My addiction affects me physically in the following ways:

_____

_____

My addiction affects me emotionally in the following ways:

_____

_____

My addiction affects me financially in the following ways:

_____

_____

My addiction affects my relationships and social life in the

following ways: _____

_____

My addiction affects me in my relationship with God in the

following ways: _____

_____

Addiction #2: _____

My addiction affects me physically in the following ways:

_____

_____

My addiction affects me emotionally in the following ways:

_____

_____

My addiction affects me financially in the following ways:

_____

_____

My addiction affects my relationships and social life in the

following ways: _____

_____

My addiction affects me in my relationship with God in the

following ways: _____

_____

Addiction #3: _____

My addiction affects me physically in the following ways:

_____

_____

My addiction affects me emotionally in the following ways:

_____

_____

My addiction affects me financially in the following ways:

_____

_____

My addiction affects my relationships and social life in the

following ways: _____

_____

My addiction affects me in my relationship with God in the

following ways: _____

_____

Addiction #4: _____

My addiction affects me physically in the following ways:

_____

_____

My addiction affects me emotionally in the following ways:

_____

_____

My addiction affects me financially in the following ways:

_____

_____

My addiction affects my relationships and social life in the

following ways: _____

_____

My addiction affects me in my relationship with God in the

following ways: _____

_____

5. GUILT AND SHAME

We are all imperfect. We all have God-given guilt and shame. Both are important in helping us realize our need for forgiveness and reconciliation with our loving Father. However, most of us experience false guilt from unhealthy relationships that obscures the true guilt that leads us back to God. When guilt collides with shame it becomes self-hatred. Then we begin to make self-destructive decisions. Working from a base of shame and feeling unlovable is often what keeps us in unhealthy codependent relationships.

Lucy was everybody's mother. All of her daughter's friends thought Alicia was lucky to have a mom like Lucy. But Alicia didn't agree. Sure, it was nice to have a mother who cared, but Lucy was absolutely smothering—she wanted to be actively involved in every area of Alicia's sixteen-year-old life. While Lucy was in treatment for codependency she discovered the base of shame that drove her compulsion to love and nurture. Lucy's treatment included a relationship history/inventory which brought into focus her neglected childhood. Her parents had consistently withheld the nurturance she needed as a child. Her shame involved facing the fact that she was the kind of woman who could withhold nurturance, just as her parents had done to her.

Lucy's shame was compounded by the following incident. One day she noticed some cute puppies abandoned near the grocery store. In her typical rescuing style, she picked up a sweet puppy and took it home. On the way home she began to worry about her husband's reaction to one more pet; she had already rescued three dogs and two cats. Finally, fear overtook her. Instead of bringing the puppy home, she drove it to a vacant area and left it there with no means of survival. Lucy harbored terrible guilt over that secret. She felt incredible shame about admitting that she was the kind of woman who could abandon a helpless, needy animal, just as she herself had been abandoned.

What actions, attitudes, or events create the most shame in you? *(For instance, I am the kind of person who can scream at and hit my children; I am ashamed of the fact that I am utterly inadequate to meet my family's needs; I'm so compulsive about buying clothes that I have actually stolen grocery money to do it.)*

_____

_____

_____

_____

The solution to shame is to receive God's acceptance. Lucy finally admitted her secret in group therapy, and she realized that she could still be accepted. No one approved of her behavior. Some even stated that she could have taken the puppy back where she found it. But everyone could accept the fact that Lucy had a dark side and that she wasn't always a good care-giver.

God knows the following shameful things about me *(for instance, that I am capable of deserting someone helpless; that I have been a child beater)*

_____

_____

and is still willing to forgive and accept me into his family.

Now that I have admitted my shame to God and received His acceptance, I will share my shame with *(name a trusted friend)*

_____ and receive his/her acceptance, too.

Now we have completed your painful cycle of addiction. Picture it graphically by filling each element of the cycle below. Begin by writing the name of a person you are codependent with in the blank by number two. Then write in your anesthesia, the consequences, your guilt and shame, and the pain that results.

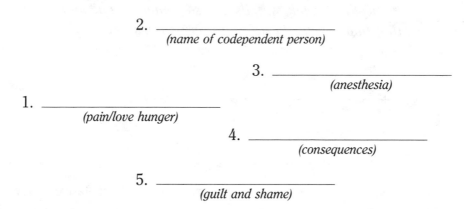

2. _____
   (name of codependent person)

3. _____
   (anesthesia)

1. _____
   (pain/love hunger)

4. _____
   (consequences)

5. _____
   (guilt and shame)

THE SPIRAL EFFECT

When the cycles of addiction start in motion, they feed off their own power. As the subject becomes conditioned to the anesthetic, larger doses are required. These lead to amplified consequences. The spiral spins downward, out of control.

In George's case, his mother truly appreciated and counted on all the time and help he gave her. But their relationship was never satisfying. She wanted more and more of his time, and he felt more and more guilt about abandoning his family. Finally George and his mother had a terrible fight. After that, she refused to see or speak to him. Shortly thereafter she suffered a stroke. George could only blame himself. He really hit bottom—his life had spiraled out of control.

Have your addictions gotten worse?　_____ yes _____ no

How? *(For instance, I wanted to help others, but now I spend all my free time volunteering for charitable organizations; I used to be happy buying a new piece of jewelry, but now I come home with two or three new outfits each time I shop.)*

1. _____

_____

2. _____

_____

3. _____

_____

4. _____

_____

BOUNDARIES

Many times codependents don't know how to set appropriate boundaries in their relationships. Boundaries are the natural limits that are part of all healthy relationships, allowing a sense of personal space and integrity. All humans are limited. Although we can touch and fill one another's love tanks, we cannot fill them perfectly or completely. Only God can do that. People with healthy relationships know and understand this reality.

Examples of Healthy Boundaries

- I care about you, but I cannot make your problems go away.
- I need to balance my time socializing with time alone.
- I am a person of worth; therefore, I don't deserve to be the target of your rage.
- I enjoy being with you, but I don't have to go out of my way to make contact with you every day.
- I want to hear and understand your opinions, but my thoughts and opinions are important too.
- I am not responsible for your emotions.
- I am responsible for my own emotions.

For each of your codependent relationships, write one healthy boundary that you need to establish. *(For instance, I need to tell*

Jerry that it's not appropriate to monopolize my evenings telling me about his problems on the phone; I need to realize that my son is his own person, and not try to rush in and fix everything in his life.)

1. _____

_____

2. _____

_____

3. _____

_____

4. _____

_____

ABSTINENCE

When something has become an addiction in your life, abstinence is the best solution. Make a choice of abstinence today about the cycles of addiction you have uncovered. Look at the example of how George would complete this exercise. Then apply it to your own addictions.

Addiction: *Helping my mother*

I will abstain from this addiction by:

- Explaining to her that I will limit my visits to one evening a week.
- Asking my wife to share the responsibility by visiting Mother once each week.

- Arranging to have a trusted handyman meet some of Mother's "emergencies."

Addiction #1: _____

I will abstain from this addiction by:

_____

_____

_____

_____

Addiction #2: _____

I will abstain from this addiction by:

_____

_____

_____

_____

Addiction #3: _____

I will abstain from this addiction by:

_____

_____

_____

_____

Addiction #4: _____

I will abstain from this addiction by:

_____

_____

_____

_____

Summary

Addictions develop a very powerful hold on our lives. It is unrealistic to plan to conquer an addiction on your own. You need supportive allies. You know that you have one in your heavenly Father. You also need a friend who will hold you accountable for the abstinence plans you developed in the previous step.

I realize that I need the support of a mature, trustworthy friend. I

will call _____ today and ask

for support in conquering my addiction cycles.

Congratulations! You have made some giant strides toward recovery.

12. Leaving Home and Saying Goodbye

A key step in recovering from codependency sounds so simple—leaving home. Why, nothing to it, right? Everyone does that. Wrong. The truth is that many people spend the majority of their lives trying to accomplish the task of leaving home. This difficult process involves untangling ourselves emotionally from the expectations put on us and the security given by our parents. There are two separate steps in the process: one is genuinely leaving the family of origin and saying goodbye to Mom and Dad. The second is giving up false security symbols. Neither step is easy.

Even if your parents are deceased, you may not have effectively said goodbye. The kind of goodbye we're dealing with in this chapter involves much more than putting physical and financial distance between you and your parents. The statements in the following checklist will help you determine if you have truly left home.

_____ I talk to one or both of my parents more than once a week.
_____ You could say my parents and I don't talk at all.
_____ I feel guilty when I don't visit or talk to my parents.
_____ I have broken all ties with my parents.

_____ My spouse or close friend accuses me of being more involved with my parents than our family or my current life.

_____ When I'm with my parents, I feel like I have to walk on eggshells.

_____ I still need my parents' approval more than anyone else's.

_____ I always have to prove myself to my parents.

_____ I have no contact with my parents.

If you checked two or more of these statements, this chapter will be an important one for you. You must let go of your anger and bitterness toward your parents, and of needing their approval. Both bitterness toward parents and lack of boundaries with them are evidence that you have not completed this important step of leaving home and saying goodbye. The following exercises are designed to assist you in this important task.

Inventory of Family Connections

I am financially and emotionally dependent on Mom in these ways *(for instance, she has helped me pay my bills several times. I buy her expensive gifts even when it puts a burden on my family. I can't make a decision without consulting her):*

_____

_____

_____

_____

I am financially and emotionally dependent on Dad in these ways *(for instance, I'm always nervous about telling him about a major decision. I depend on him to fix my car):*

_____

_____

_____

_____

Mom is financially and emotionally dependent on me in these ways *(for instance, she acts hurt if I don't call her every day)*:

_____

_____

_____

Dad is financially and emotionally dependent on me in these ways *(for instance, he tries to manipulate my life by offering and withholding money)*:

_____

_____

_____

My contact with Mom is obsessive and unnecessary when *(for instance, she insists that I "call in" whenever I get home after an outing)*

_____

_____

_____

_____

My contact with Dad is obsessive and unnecessary when *(for instance, I become so involved with taking care of his problems that I can't have a life of my own)*

_____

_____

_____

_____

I get my fix from Mom by *(for instance, pleasing her so she will shower me with praise and appreciation)*

_____

_____

_____

_____

I get my fix from Dad by *(for instance, needing his verbal abuse to put me in my place because someday I really will be able to please him)*

_____

_____

_____

_____

I don't associate with Mom because *(for instance, the relationship has been so painful, I just decided to cut it off)*

_____

_____

_____

_____

I don't associate with Dad because *(for instance, every time I talk to him, I want to get back at him somehow)*

_____

_____

_____

_____

Is the picture of your dependencies on your parents becoming clearer? _____ yes _____ no

Looking back over this exercise, summarize the ways you have not left home. *(For instance, I still look too much to my father for approval. My financial dependency gives my parents too much power over me. I still feel responsible for my parents' feelings.)*

1. _____

_____

2. _____

_____

3. _____

_____

4. _____

5. _____

BREAKING OUT OF ROLES

In chapter 9 you identified the roles you played in your family of origin. Learning to deal with how these roles have affected your adult life will help you accomplish the task of leaving home and saying goodbye. Let's briefly review the roles that appear in dysfunctional families.

Hero: has a responsible personality; is rewarded for good behavior and good work; often takes over parental roles.

Scapegoat: is seen as rebellious by the family and is often blamed for family problems.

Mascot: gets attention by being cute and funny; tries to laugh and joke the pain away.

Lost child: is a loner; tries to stay away from attention for fear it will be negative; is usually liked by others, but rarely noticed.

It's very possible that as an adult you may be continuing to play the same role you played as a child. Such was the case with one young man, named Jim, who received counseling at our clinic. He had grown up in the shadow of a father who was a financial failure. As a child Jim had compensated by playing the role of hero. As an adult he became an outrageous workaholic in a subconscious effort to carry on his hero role and somehow redeem his family of origin through his own good works.

Some people react strongly *against* their former role and assume a dramatically contrasting part in their adult life. Rick, a minister's son, is a good example. He spent his childhood and teen years playing the hero and living up to the expectations placed on him by his family and the members of the church. After living in a fishbowl for twenty years, he suddenly embraced the opposite lifestyle, drinking heavily, running around with wild friends, and going through a series of shallow sexual relationships. This is his way of reacting or rebelling against the role he was designated to play for so many years.

The key question for you is this: As an adult, are you mimicking the role you played as a child, or are you rebelling against it? Either position will leave you in bondage. Working through the following exercise will help you identify your present-day roles.

Today I most often find myself playing the role of *(circle one or more):*

hero   scapegoat   mascot   lost child

This is shown in the fact that *(for instance, I try to rescue anyone close to me who gets in trouble; I enjoy living on the wild side, so people blame me when things go wrong)*

_____

_____

Check and/or complete the statements that apply to you.

_____ The role I am playing today is mimicking the role I played as a child.

_____ I can see where, over the course of my lifetime, I have participated in the following roles *(for instance, I was the mascot until my older brother left home—then I became the scapegoat):*

_____

_____

_____ At the time I made the shift in roles, I knew that I was doing it to rebel.

_____ At the time I made the shift, I had no idea that I was, in reality, rebelling.

_____ I feel that the role I play today is something I'm driven to do, but I'm not always sure why.

_____ I wish I understood why I have this need to play the part

of the _____

_____ I find myself playing one role at work and another at home or with friends.

Acknowledging that your unchosen childhood role is affecting your current behavior—either because you are still mimicking that role or because you have rebelled against it—is an important start. But your goal is to fully free yourself from the influence of those old roles. This may involve actually grieving over the loss of the old role. For example, if you've spent your whole life as a sacrificing hero only to realize that you can't rescue your family after all, you may well experience a sense of grief. That grief will result from acknowledging the fact that your overachievement can't really help your loved ones after all. You'll also need to grieve over the personal loss and pain you've experienced as the designated hero.

Having identified your role in your family of origin, what function were you called upon to perform for your family? *(For instance, as the family mascot I was designated the one to distract everyone from pain. As the lost child I was designated the one to stay out of the way and take care of myself.)*

As the family _____, I was designated the

one to _____

Did your commitment to your role resolve any of the pain or shame in your family of origin? _____ yes _____ no

What did your commitment to your role do to you? *(For instance, because I concentrated on staying out of the way, it has become difficult for me to get close to people. My hero role turned me into a workaholic with chronic health problems.)*

_____

_____

_____

When I was caught up in playing my role as a child, I often felt *(for instance, a sense of desperation; that I was the last person to be able to avert disaster; trapped—that I couldn't get out of this role if I wanted to)*

_____

_____

_____

As a child, my commitment to my role cost me the freedom to be who I wanted to be; it also cost me *(for instance, my childhood; learning how to create balance in my life; the freedom to express my true feelings)*

_____

_____

As an adult, I can see how the ongoing influence of my childhood role has affected me in a negative way. One example is *(for instance, then I was the hero, now I've become a workaholic; I still feel responsible for things that are beyond my influence)*

_____

_____

When I think about these losses that I have experienced as a child and as an adult, I feel *(for instance, sad that I've been put under so much pressure by these roles; angry that I continue to play the roles today even though they hurt me)*

_____

_____

_____

The unwanted roles I still play from my childhood are *(circle one):*

mascot   hero   scapegoat   lost child

If I were starting over with a clean slate and could make decisions about my life totally free from the influence of my past roles, I would make the decision to change *(for instance, my compulsion to take care of everybody; the need to hide my true feelings from people by always making them laugh)*

_____

_____

_____

_____

It's only when you have examined, grieved over, and released unwanted roles from your childhood that you will have removed a significant source of the pain that fuels your codependency. Only then will you be able to make new decisions and give yourself permission to select new, more appropriate roles.

A LETTER HOME

A method we often use in counseling to help patients leave home and say goodbye is to have them write letters to their parents. When you write a letter that you don't plan to send, you can get out feelings that have been festering for a long time. If the parent is deceased, of course, the letter can never be sent. But if you're writing to a living parent, you have the choice of rewriting it in a milder form and sending it to your parent or parents.

Use this space to write a letter to your parents. Under no circumstances will you send this letter—this exercise is for your benefit only. Be as expressive and honest as possible. Tell of your feelings of love and tenderness, anger and bitterness, frustration, admiration—all of it. In nearly every case, patients find that writing this letter unleashes memories and emotions that are very important to their recovery. (If you are an adopted child, write letters to all parents, adopted and biological.)

Dear Mom,

_____

_____

_____

_____

_____

_____

_____

_____

_____

_____

_____

_____

_____

_____

_____

Dear Dad,

_____

_____

_____

_____

_____

_____

_____

_____

_____

_____

_____

_____

_____

_____

(Use more paper if needed.)

If you feel that it's important to send your letter, then rewrite it in a milder, more tactful form. The purpose of sending the letter will be to express your feelings in a constructive way that will help your parent understand your pain, your commitment to recovery, and your new choice of roles.

Summary

Writing letters such as these is not meant to dishonor your parents. If you write a second draft that you are actually going to send, it should not insult or belittle the parent you're addressing. It is an honest description of hurts, not a condemnation. It may contain praise where praise is due.

The greatest honor you can give your parents is to become the person God intended you to be. If unfinished business and other emotional baggage are hindering your growth, then it's important that you shed that baggage. Writing the letter to your parents will help you do that. Be loving but firm, and get it behind you.

We need to close this chapter with a word of warning. There is a sad paradox in this leaving-home concept. Codependents, the persons most in need of putting the original family behind them, have the greatest difficulty making the break. Goodbyes and transitions are never easy, even for an emotionally healthy child. The first day of school, graduation, and marriage may all bring a tear or two. Such events are poignant, but do-able. Healthy families release each other. But appropriate goodbyes are difficult, bordering on impossible, for persons emerging from a painful, dysfunctional, abusive childhood. This is why the next lesson will take you through the grieving process.

13. GRIEVING YOUR LOSS

We promised you at the beginning of these ten stages of recovery that the first part of your journey would resemble the downward plunge of a roller-coaster ride. Then we proceeded to take you on a guided tour of your pain—pain from past events, unhealthy relationships, addictions and their consequences, and finally the pain of leaving the secure, if unhappy, roles you've played. It's likely that you've already begun to feel the weight of these losses. Here is the good news: Things get better from here. This is the bottom of the curve. But before you start on the upswing, you need to take time for grief.

"Good grief" may seem like a paradoxical expression. But, in fact, it makes a lot of sense. It's important to learn how to grieve well, because your losses will continue to affect your life until you have grieved for them fully and appropriately. Grief is especially important to the adult child who is codependent, who needs powerfully and emotionally to grieve for all the losses brought to awareness in stages one through four of the recovery process. It is very important to grieve the details of loss from childhood through your present relationships. The goal of this chapter is to help you develop a system for dealing with grief that will serve you both now and in dealing with future losses.

The grief process, pioneered by Elisabeth Kübler-Ross and now common knowledge among psychologists, is a largely spontaneous chain of events and feelings. The stages through which every grieving person passes are (1) shock and denial, (2) anger, (3) depression, (4) bargaining and magic, and finally, (5) resolution and acceptance. To that progression we have added another step. In our frame of reference, sadness becomes number five, moving resolution and acceptance to six.

What Are My Losses?

Many codependents have no idea that they need to grieve. Before we give you exercises to acknowledge your grief, take a moment to identify the major painful losses that have left a mark on your life. It is very likely that these losses appear in your Relationship History/Inventory in chapter 9. They may include such things as the death of a special pet, divorce, loss of a best friend who moved away, the termination of a once close relationship, or the loss of a physical ability.

What are the major losses you need to grieve?

1. _____

2. _____

3. _____

4. _____

5. _____

6. _____

7. _____

8. _____

9. _____

10. _____

Some losses aren't as obvious as others. Silly as it sounds, you may need to grieve for certain aspects of your healing as well. Your addictive behaviors and feelings once occupied a very significant part of your life. Now they are banished, and a very big empty space is left behind. Grief is appropriate for something that once meant so much to you. In particular, after the previous chapter's work of untangling unhealthy emotional ties with your parents, you must grieve the loss of the pain you lived with for so long. Good riddance, perhaps, but what an empty hole it leaves.

Think a moment about all the things you lose when you give up your codependency. The first thing to go is your false sense of security. George, the adult son from the last chapter, was miserably codependent on his mother. But there was security in his misery. He knew that every week he would spend a great deal of time tending to her needs. He didn't even have to explore any other options; he just kept going home to Mother. The next thing that goes out the door with your codependency is the feeling of being needed. George may have felt like a first-class failure as a husband and father, but he could feel absolutely secure in the fact that his mother would always need and appreciate him. Many codependents thrive on filling their time by meeting others' needs. This was certainly true in George's case. By taking care of Mom he could avoid the problems in his marriage. That avoidance also goes out the door with codependency. You can see the tremendous sense of loss George felt as he progressed through the recovery process and left these familiar, if unhealthy, patterns behind. You may be feeling it, too. What will you lose if you give up your codependency?

_____ my false sense of security
_____ my feeling of being needed
_____ the ability to fill my time meeting others' needs
_____ the ability to avoid my own pain

Identifying Personal Losses

It's very likely that your codependency has caused losses in every area of your life. Let's identify some of those losses.

Your Family Life

_____ I have repeated the negative patterns I learned as a child in my married family.

_____ I have never married, largely because of my codependent problems.

_____ My marriage is in a shambles because of codependent issues between my husband and me.

_____ I can see how my children have suffered from my codependent behaviors as a parent.

_____ My workaholism has nearly destroyed my family life.

_____ *(other)* _____

_____

Your Career

_____ I've never been able to follow my own dreams because I felt I had to fulfill my parents' goals for me.

_____ Personal problems in relationships have prevented me from advancing in my job.

_____ My addictions have adversely affected my work performance.

_____ I find it difficult to stand up for myself when I am criticized at work.

_____ *(other)* _____

_____

Your Spiritual Life

_____ I never developed a relationship with God because I imagined that He was harsh and judgmental like my father.

_____ My sense of self-worth has always been so low that I couldn't imagine being worthy of Christ's love.

_____ After the treatment I got at home, it's been hard for me to trust anybody—including God.

_____ I have always blamed God for the problems in my life, instead of blaming my codependency.

_____ _(other)_ _____

_____

If you checked even one of those statements, you have suffered a major loss, and you have some legitimate grieving to do.

The Six Stages of Grief

No one goes through grief in a straightforward, lockstep manner. Many of our patients at the clinic have worked through part of the grief cycle, only to "get stuck" at a certain point and fail to bring their grief to a satisfactory conclusion. These exercises will help you define where you are in your grieving process, and show you how to move on.

1. SHOCK AND DENIAL

Psychologists believe that many codependents and adult children walk around in a chronic state of emotional shock, similar to the first step in the grieving process. They get hung up at the very beginning and aren't able to get on with their healing. Denial is so strong with them that they spend their lives in a kind of posthypnotic trance. That's why the first four steps of healing have all focused on accepting the reality of your dysfunctional family and getting in touch with your pain.

In what areas of your life have you been able to completely break through shock and denial? *(For instance, I've admitted my addiction to taking financial risks; I've admitted that my perfectionism is based in fear of being unlovable and that it's causing a lot of problems in my family.)*

1. _____

_____

2. _____

_____

3. _____

_____

There may be some painful issues in your life that you're still covering with shock and denial. This exercise is designed to help you bring those issues out in the open.

I still find it hard to believe that *(for instance, I wasn't to blame for the misery in our home; my father's lack of interest in me was actually passive abuse)*

_____

_____

Sometimes I feel as if it wasn't even me who *(for instance, was molested by Uncle Nick)*

_____

_____

One abuse I wrote down was _____

_____,

but it wasn't really as bad as it sounds because _____

_____

2. ANGER

Following almost immediately behind shock and denial comes anger. To test this statement in everyday life, imagine if you were to run up to someone and stomp on his foot. His first reaction would be shock: "What . . . ?" The next would be "That didn't really happen, did it?" Then comes anger: "Who do you think you are, doing that to me!" All those thoughts may flash through his mind in the few moments before he retaliates against you. However prolonged or momentary, those steps in the process happen.

Perhaps breaking out of shock and denial has left you feeling angry. We're not surprised. It's so much a part of the grieving process that even people who lose spouses to accidental deaths feel anger that the spouse has gone off and left them alone.

Name five people you've felt especially angry with as you've worked through the exercises in this book.

1. _____

2. _____

3. _____

4. _____

5. _____

I still blame _____ for the fact that I

_____

_____

The one person I'm going to have a hard time forgiving is _____

_____

If God really cared about me, he _____

_____

_____

I'm really angry with _____ for

_____

_____

If you've been unable to answer the preceding questions, it doesn't mean you don't have anger. It probably means that you have spent a lifetime trying to make others comfortable and happy, and in the process you've trained yourself to suppress your anger.

Remember, anger is a natural, healthy, God-given emotional mechanism for dealing with pain and loss. Feeling anger does not make you a bad person—it makes you normal. If you haven't acknowledged your anger to this point, do it now. There is good evidence that deeply held and repressed anger can suppress the immune system of the body. You need to get that "toxic waste" out of your system.

3. DEPRESSION

Serious depression disorders occur in people who turn their anger inward. When anger goes underground, the resulting deep depression or numbness can last a lifetime. Healing is nearly impossible under those conditions. "Oh, great!" you're thinking. "All this, and depression, too?"

We want to reassure you right from the start that the kind of depression we're talking about in the grieving process is temporary. It resolves itself.

We often see patients in the clinic who have a very difficult time breaking through denial. Once they finally acknowledge their pain they may literally weep and wail for days. Walter Morgan, a perfectionistic pastor who came in for treatment when his life crumbled, was like that. After he was finally able to express his anger, he languished in a deep depression. But he emerged spontaneously from his depression, as do the vast majority of people going through the grieving process.

I find it depressing to be around the following people:

1. _____

2. _____

3. _____

I often get depressed in these situations:

1. _____

2. _____

3. _____

When I think about _____,

it makes me wonder if there's any hope at all for the future.

The last time I got really depressed, it was about _____

_____

_____

_____

If you find yourself hung up at the depression point, go back through the preceding steps and make sure you have truly acknowledged your loss and anger. Then you will be ready to progress through the healing process.

4. BARGAINING AND MAGIC

Bargaining and magic are tricks we use to try to hustle ourselves out of a bad situation. Who has not, in desperation, tried to bargain with God by saying, "God, if you'll only get me out of this mess, I'll. . . ."? We use bargains to try to get an edge against our pain, so that we can go around it instead of through it.

Magical thinking centers around "If only . . ." statements. It's a very natural part of childhood. "If only I were prettier, Daddy would love me more and stop hitting me." The codependent adult carries this kind of invalid, illogical thinking to extremes. Work through this list of statements that reflect bargaining and magical thinking, and check those that resemble thoughts you have had.

_____ God, if you show me a way out of this problem, I promise to straighten out my life and serve you.

_____ If only I were thinner, people would love me, and all my problems would be solved.

_____ If I try hard enough and do well in my job, my father will be pleased with me and give me his approval at last.

_____ If only my children would behave decently, I wouldn't have to scream at them all the time.

_____ If only I could be the perfect wife, my husband would finally appreciate me.

_____ If only I can buy the house of my dreams, I'll finally be happy.

_____ If I can stay away from sex entirely, I won't have to deal with the abuse from my past.

_____ If only I can excel at my work, I can make up for the pain of my mother's rejection.

I have promised myself that I will never _____

_____

I told God that if He would _____

_____, then I would _____

_____

Has this exercise made you realize some of your own bargains?
_____ yes _____ no

What are they? *(For instance, after my first marriage ended, I promised myself I'd never let anyone hurt me again.)*

_____

_____

_____

Are you willing to give up your bargains and magical thinking?
_____ yes _____ no

5. SADNESS

Sadness is normal. Sadness is ordinary. Sadness is the appropriate response to sad events. Best of all, sadness is not endless. Unlike chronic depression, repetition, and suppressed anger, sadness comes, is recognized, and goes. This is when you settle down for a good, old-fashioned cry. You may want to cry alone, but at times you might find it very helpful to do your crying on a sympathetic shoulder.

Give yourself time at this stage; don't look for any quick fixes. There's a lot of wisdom in the old saying, "A good cry cleanses the soul." Visualize your tears washing away your pain. And remember, God is always accessible. Let yourself be gathered into the comfort of his presence.

I feel brokenhearted when I think about _____

_____

_____

I can acknowledge that tears can be a good thing, and I give myself permission to cry. _____ yes _____ no

The last time I had a really good cry was _____

_____

_____

During my recovery, I have already felt genuine sadness about:

1. _____

2. _____

3. _____

6. FORGIVENESS, RESOLUTION, AND ACCEPTANCE

This is the point at which you can stop and heave a big sigh of relief. The hardest work is behind you. Peace and freedom are within reach. The painful issues of the past no longer have control over you.

It hasn't come easily, has it? In order to achieve forgiveness, resolution, and acceptance, you have to do a thorough job at each of the previous stages. At the Minirth-Meier Clinics we find that many persons try to forgive without acknowledging and working through their anger, depression, and sadness. Unfortunately, this leaves these toxic feelings trapped inside them.

Name five people you've identified as needing your forgiveness as you've gone through this workbook.

1. _____

2. _____

3. _____

4. _____

5. _____

One by one, visualize these people in your mind. Can you say, "I forgive you," to each one of them, and do it with perfect peace of mind? _____ yes _____ no _____ not yet, but I'm working on it

Where are you in the forgiveness process with each of these people? Write the appropriate number by each name in your list above.

1. I'm still in shock and denial.
2. I haven't yet fully acknowledged and expressed my anger.
3. I've reached the point of depression.
4. I'm still dealing with bargaining and magical thinking.
5. I've been crying out my sadness.
6. I have accepted what's happened and forgiven this person; I am at peace.

Forgiveness isn't logical from a human standpoint, but, the fact is, it works. It brings the release and acceptance that enable you to get on with your life. In order to achieve true forgiveness, you may need to recycle through the stages of the healing process. You may need to do it more than once. And you may need to ask God's help.

Remember, you're not excusing what was done to you; you're accepting the fact that it happened and offering forgiveness as God's solution to your pain. Once you've accomplished this, that person will no longer have power over you, and you will find God's "peace that passes understanding."

I can't change the fact that _____

_____; I can see that the way to release

my pain is to _____

_____

I'm willing to let go of _____

_____

_____

One thought that is especially freeing for me is _____

_____

_____

_____

I forgive God for _____

_____

_____

I forgive my parents for _____

_____

_____

I forgive myself for _____

_____

_____

_____

For the first time I feel a sense of peace about _____

_____

_____

_____

Summary

It's unrealistic to expect yourself to have completely worked through your grief by the end of this chapter. Grief follows its own timetable. And it's not a strictly linear process—you may be all the way up to sadness, then one day find yourself flopping back to anger. This is normal. Have patience with yourself and realize that each time you recycle, the process becomes a little easier. And one day you *will* be done with it.

The important thing is not to allow yourself to get hung up at any one point. If you can't seem to get through a certain stage, then try one of these strategies:

- Write a letter expressing your anger.
- Ask God to help you see the other person as a fellow sufferer and give you the grace and strength to forgive.
- Stop bargaining and accept your loss.
- Allow yourself some crying time.
- Share your sadness with a friend.

And the peace of God, which surpasses all understanding, will guard your hearts and minds through Christ Jesus. (Phil. 4:7)

14. New Self-Perceptions

If you grew up in a dysfunctional home, you inevitably carry an assortment of negative, distorted messages. These messages play over and over in your head, controlling your life and coloring your perceptions. To a severely codependent person, internalized negative messages may be so vicious and penetrating that the simple thought, "I have permission to live," may come as a welcome revelation.

Jennifer, the perfectionistic wife and mother from chapter 1, has internalized a set of negative messages like this:

- I can be valuable only if I'm doing things for other people.
- If I keep running I won't need to face the fact that I'm basically worthless.
- I can't let other people see how bad I really am.
- I'm trying to make my children's lives better than mine, but I don't think I'm succeeding.

As part of her recovery, Jennifer identified these negative messages and learned to counter them with new, positive thoughts like these:

- My worth as a person is not based on what I do.
- I can face myself and accept the fact that there is both good and bad in me.
- Other people can know my faults and still accept me.
- I will be the best mother I can be, and I'll leave the rest up to God.

Stages one through five of the recovery process have brought you in touch with your feelings, perhaps for the first time. The exercises in this workbook have given you an opportunity for catharsis and renewal. Now in stages six through ten, we'll work at cleaning out more unhealthy toxins, then we'll fill the void left by damaged and damaging thoughts. If that void is left empty, it will almost certainly fill itself with negative attitudes and thoughts, for old habits die hard. In other words, it's time to teach the old dog a few new tricks. Welcome to the new you!

Read over this list and check the statements that apply to you.

_____ I am unloved.
_____ I am unlovable, even in the eyes of God.
_____ I'm responsible for everyone else's hurt and pain.
_____ I'm not worthy, so I need to earn my way into salvation and grace, both in my family and in the greater family of God.
_____ I don't deserve this success I'm having.

Getting in Touch with Old Perceptions

In order to defuse old, damaging messages, you first need to realize exactly what they are.

Some of my negative perceptions about life in general are
(for instance, happiness is always just out of my reach; I can always count on the worst thing happening)

_____

_____

_____

_____

Some of my negative perceptions about other people are *(for instance, people are always out to get me; the best way to keep from getting hurt is to avoid developing close relationships)*

_____

_____

_____

_____

Some of my negative perceptions about my personality, abilities, and appearance are *(for instance, because I'm unattractive, no one can like me; my opinions don't really matter)*

_____

_____

_____

_____

Finish the following statements to reflect your old perceptions. Remember, be candid with yourself. Most of us carry around some strong generalizations which may or may not fit reality.

All women are _____

_____

All men are _____

_____

God is _____

_____

All people are _____

_____

A home should be _____

_____

I am _____

_____

My life is _____

_____

The world will never be _____

_____

Good things like _____

_____ will never happen to me.

Out with the Old, In with the New

Therefore, if anyone is in Christ, he is a new creation; old things have passed away; behold, all things have become new. (2 Cor. 5:17)

It's time to put on a whole new set of perceptions. For each of the negative thoughts you expressed above, write the opposite, positive thought. If there are any positive statements that you want to keep, rewrite them in an even more positive manner.

Some new perceptions about life in general are *(for instance, I can anticipate both joy and pain in my life; because God is a loving Father, I don't need to fear what lies ahead)*

_____

_____

_____

_____

Some new perceptions about other people are *(for instance, while I've had some negative experiences, many people have been kind and loving to me; I can make wise choices in my relationships)*

_____

_____

_____

_____

Some new perceptions about my personality, abilities, and appearance are *(for instance, I have many likeable qualities; I am a person of worth and my opinions are important)*

_____

_____

_____

Finish the following statements to reflect your new perceptions.

Some women are _____

_____

Some men are _____

_____

God is _____

_____

Some people are _____

_____

A home could be _____

_____

I am _____

_____

My life is _____

_____

The world can be _____

_____

Good things like _____

_____ will happen to me.

Believe It

Once you've established a series of new messages, you'll need to play them over and over in your mind. It may take a while before they become real to you. The old perceptions you're trying to break away from didn't develop overnight; they came from years of reinforcement in your unhealthy family environment. Now you need to practice reinforcement of your new messages, so that they become as strongly influential in your life as your old messages once were.

Rewrite these negative messages into positive ones.

I can't be okay unless I have everyone's approval.

_____

_____

God won't love me unless I do something to earn His love.

_____

_____

I must be perfect.

_____

_____

A good Christian should meet all the needs of others.

_____

_____

I will die if I try to face my pain.

_____

_____

My spouse should meet all my needs.

_____

_____

Expressing feelings is a sign of weakness.

_____

_____

I shouldn't feel angry, hurt, or depressed.

_____

_____

The world would be better off without me.

_____

_____

My family can't handle my negative feelings.

_____

_____

I can never be happy.

_____

_____

I will never feel safe and cared for.

_____

_____

I have to make life work on my own.

_____

_____

I can't trust anyone.

_____

_____

My world would fall apart if I let myself feel.

_____

_____

I have no right to my anger.

_____

_____

I don't count.

_____

_____

I don't matter to anyone.

_____

_____

My life has been a total waste.

_____

_____

Developing Realistic Expectations

The world isn't a perfect place. There will always be some kind of pain or sorrow to face, even after you've recovered from codependency. Your new perceptions need to include ways to deal with the hurtful things life throws at you without developing negative self-perceptions. It's important to learn how to live with disappointment without blaming yourself or taking on unhealthy internal messages.

First, consider the expectations you have for yourself and significant others in your life. Mark an "H" by the expectations you think are healthy, and a "U" by the ones you consider to be unhealthy.

My expectations for myself include:

1. _____ I will not make major mistakes.
2. _____ I have to meet everyone's needs.
3. _____ When people are angry with me, I won't run and hide.
4. _____ I will protect the people in my world from getting hurt.
5. _____ I will do my best for those I care about, but I can't make things perfect for them.
6. _____ I can win everyone's approval.
7. _____ I will never let anybody down.
8. _____ Nobody will ever get mad at me.
9. _____ I can have down days.
10. _____ I don't have to be perfect.
11. _____ I'll do my best to be a friend, but I don't expect everyone to like me.

My expectations for significant others in my life include:

1. _____ They will always be sensitive to all of my needs.
2. _____ They are helpless and can't do anything without me.
3. _____ They can't ever be mad at me.
4. _____ They are responsible for their own lives, and I'll hurt them if I try to take care of everything for them.
5. _____ They will meet some of my needs.
6. _____ If they get angry at me, that doesn't mean the end of the world or of the relationship.
7. _____ Our relationship will have its ups and downs, but we'll remain committed to each other.
8. _____ Their expectations of me are always right.
9. _____ My opinions have equal importance with theirs.

The healthy responses in the first group are numbers 3, 5, 9, 10, and 11. In the second group the healthy responses are 4, 5, 6, 7, and 9.

Share your lists of old and new perceptions with a trusted friend or support group. Choose someone who will be your ally as you retrain your thinking to reflect a positive attitude about life.

You may find it helpful to write your new messages on note cards, and put them up around your house in places where you'll see them often. Rehearse them over and over in your mind, until they really become part of you.

> Whatever things are true, whatever things are noble, whatever things are just, whatever things are pure, whatever things are lovely, whatever things are of good report, if there is any virtue and if there is anything praiseworthy—meditate on these things . . . and the God of peace will be with you. (Phil. 4:8–9b)

15. NEW EXPERIENCES

As you've worked through this book, you've discovered what a tremendous impact your past experiences have had on your present situation. You've worked hard to understand yourself and correct the negative messages you internalized over the years. Now your new positive messages require new experiences to confirm them. The next step in your recovery is to create new experiences based on your new perceptions about yourself, other people, and life in general. These new experiences will not be bound by issues from your past.

In earlier chapters we discussed the problems of George, a codependent adult son. The negative messages George gave himself were: "My mother will die if I don't meet all of her needs"; "My wife will leave me if I don't meet all of her needs." After his mother's stroke, George talked with a counselor about his tremendous guilt feelings. The counselor helped him to come up with a new, positive message: "I can and will meet *some* of my mother's and my wife's needs." While his mother recuperated at home under the care of a nurse, George visited her twice a week and phoned her on three other days. His wife, Carol, agreed to make two separate visits as well. George's new experience was that his mother did not die—in fact, she became less demanding. His new experience with Carol was that she became happier and more secure in their marriage, knowing exactly how much time he would be spending with his mother. George could hardly believe the change in both his wife and his mother. He felt at peace and free to make choices for the first time in his life.

All your relationships will be affected by "the new you." Beside each person or group of people below, describe the relationship you would like to have.

Spouse: *(For instance, I want to have a mutual meeting of needs; I don't want to be afraid of conflict, but able to resolve it.)*

_____

_____

Children: *(For instance, I want to be aware of their love tanks and meet the needs I'm responsible for; I want to stop smothering them.)*

_____

_____

Friends: *(For instance, I want to develop a network of support; I don't want to take responsibility for all of their problems.)*

_____

_____

Parents: *(For instance, I will honor them by regular contact but also realize I'm not responsible for their happiness; I don't want to keep seeking their approval for everything.)*

_____

_____

Siblings: *(For instance, I want to share my honest feelings with them; I want to accept them for where they are in their recovery process, even if they haven't begun.)*

_____

_____

In-laws: *(For instance, I want to encourage my spouse to have a healthy relationship with his/her parents; I don't want to let them interfere with our having a healthy, independent family.)*

_____

_____

Colleagues: *(For instance, I don't want to be dumped on or used by them; I want to be more positive toward them.)*

_____

_____

How will you need to change in order to move these relationships in a healthy direction?

Spouse: *(For instance, when I'm angry about something I will discuss it with my spouse in a calm, rational manner.)*

_____

_____

Children: *(For instance, I will read parenting books so I can know what they need at each stage of their development.)*

_____

_____

Friends: *(For instance, I will be friendly and open toward people; I won't be afraid to ask my friends for help when I need it.)*

_____

_____

Parents: *(For instance, I need to stop going to them for reassurance about every decision I make.)*

_____

_____

Siblings: *(For instance, I will have a meaningful contact with each of my siblings once a year.)*

_____

_____

In-laws: *(For instance, I will stand up to them when they try to interfere with my marriage or my children.)*

_____

_____

Colleagues: *(For instance, I will work toward establishing a friendly atmosphere at work; I will open dialogues about what my work responsibilities are so I don't feel overwhelmed.)*

_____

_____

Building Healthy New Boundaries

Every healthy relationship is sheltered by boundaries. For codependents in recovery, one of the biggest tasks is to establish strong, healthy boundaries in relationships that were formerly codependent. This requires some careful thinking and planning, especially if the other person has unresolved issues of codependency.

Let's use an example from marriage. Suppose the husband says, "I'm depressed, and it's your fault." A codependent wife's internal negative response would be, "Yes, it's my fault. No one likes to be around me. It's too bad you're stuck with me for a wife." If the wife recovers from codependency, she will establish healthy new boundaries that will permit her to say, "I understand your depression, and I hurt for you. I'm sorry. I offer you my love and support, but I won't take responsibility for your feelings. They are your province." Love has become a choice, not a demand.

Think about some of the trouble spots and tricky relationships in your life. Is there a particular aunt who always sets you off? Or a co-worker who really bugs you? You may need to set some special boundaries that will help you function securely in those relationships. Choose ten close relationships for which you need to set new boundaries. Write in the ten names in the exercise below. Then go back to each one and write about your new boundaries and how you will put them into effect. The first one is done as a sample for you.

The boundaries I need with _____ *my best friend* _____ are

I can be available for lunch one time a week; if she phones too

often, I will tell her that I can't talk right now.

I will communicate these boundaries by _____ *telling her over lunch in*

the context of appreciating her and her friendship.

If my boundaries aren't accepted, I will _____ *tell her I need to go, and*

I will hang up the phone.

   1. The boundaries I need with *(name)* _____

      are _____

_____

_____

I will communicate these boundaries by _____

_____

_____

If my boundaries are not accepted, I will _____

_____

_____

2. The boundaries I need with *(name)* _____

   are _____

   _____

   _____

   I will communicate these boundaries by _____

   _____

   _____

   If my boundaries are not accepted, I will _____

   _____

   _____

3. The boundaries I need with *(name)* _____

   are _____

_____

_____

I will communicate these boundaries by _____

_____

_____

If my boundaries are not accepted, I will _____

_____

_____

4. The boundaries I need with *(name)* _____

are _____

_____

_____

I will communicate these boundaries by _____

_____

_____

If my boundaries are not accepted, I will _____

_____

_____

5. The boundaries I need with *(name)* _____

are _____

_____

_____

I will communicate these boundaries by _____

_____

_____

If my boundaries are not accepted, I will _____

_____

_____

6. The boundaries I need with *(name)* _____

are _____

_____

_____

I will communicate these boundaries by _____

_____

_____

If my boundaries are not accepted, I will _____

_____

_____

7. The boundaries I need with *(name)* _____

are _____

_____

_____

I will communicate these boundaries by _____

_____

_____

If my boundaries are not accepted, I will _____

_____

_____

8. The boundaries I need with *(name)* _____

are _____

_____

_____

I will communicate these boundaries by _____

_____

_____

If my boundaries are not accepted, I will _____

_____

_____

9. The boundaries I need with *(name)* _____

are _____

_____

_____

I will communicate these boundaries by _____

_____

_____

If my boundaries are not accepted, I will _____

_____

_____

10. The boundaries I need with *(name)* _____

    are _____

    _____

    _____

    I will communicate these boundaries by _____

    _____

    _____

    If my boundaries are not accepted, I will _____

    _____

    _____

One word of precaution about establishing new boundaries: They may come as something of a shock to the other people involved. The people with whom you were formerly codependent will probably be surprised by the new you. When you explain the new limits of your relationship, you may run across some negative reactions. That's okay. It does not mean that your new boundaries are wrong in any way; it simply means they take some getting used to.

LOOKING AT THE NEW YOU

One of the most important new experiences for you is to affirm a new, positive view of yourself. Earlier in the book, we asked you to write a list of things you don't like about yourself. For most people, that is a remarkably easy task. Now we're going to ask you to do just the opposite. Write a list of a dozen things you like about yourself. We bet you'll find it harder to write. In fact, you might even need to get some help. This is where your support group or confidante can come in handy. If you're reluctant to admit you're likeable, let them help you along!

Things I like about myself include:

1. _____

2. _____

3. _____

4. _____

5. _____

6. _____

7. _____

8. _____

9. _____

10. _____

11. _____

12. _____

LOOKING TO THE FUTURE

Make a list of new experiences you would like to have. Don't be shy about this list. Remember, "If you reach for the roof, you may not make it; if you reach for the stars, you may get past the roof." It's absolutely true that people who have goals and plans get somewhere. They might not make it all the way to their goal, but they get *somewhere*. You can, too.

Things I would like to do in my lifetime include:

1. _____

2. _____

3. _____

4. _____

5. _____

6. _____

7. _____

8. _____

9. _____

10. _____

11. _____

12. _____

13. _____

14. _____

15. _____

A new experience I would like to have this week is *(for instance, meeting my husband for lunch and speaking openly about my feelings for the first time)*

_____

_____

_____

Once you've accomplished your new experience, tell what it felt

like. _____

_____

_____

A new experience I would like to have this month is _____

_____

_____

Once you've accomplished your new experience, tell what it felt

like. _____

_____

_____

Summary

Many of the people we work with at Minirth-Meier Clinics are totally amazed by their new experiences. Patti was sexually abused by her father. In her adult life she totally avoided any kind of emotional or sexual intimacy with men. Her old message was, "Men can't be trusted." In therapy she learned the new message that "some men can be trusted; I can make wise choices in my male friendships." Patti's counselor encouraged her toward the new experience of finding a safe man to make friends with. "It was scary at first," Patti admitted, "but I did find a man I could really talk to. It felt so neat to be sharing part of my life with someone."

We hope that you will find the courage to step out into some positive new experiences of your own. Most people are delighted and surprised to find that their new perceptions are true. We think you will be, too.

> Their souls shall be like a well-watered garden, and they shall sorrow no more at all. Then shall the virgin rejoice in the dance, and the young men and the old, together; for I will turn their mourning to joy, will comfort them, and make them rejoice rather than sorrow. (Jer. 31:12b–13)

16. REPARENTING

Deep inside there is a part of you that still thinks and reacts as a child. That emotional child will stay with you through your whole life; it's the part of you that is most sensitive to the pain of your dysfunctional family. As you've worked through this book and gotten in touch with that emotional child, you've probably found the pain to be as fresh as the day it happened. There are some steps you need to take to nurture and heal the child within you. This process is called reparenting.

Reparenting fills in the deficits of your original upbringing. You can't go back home and demand that your parents make everything up to you. But you can find new sources to fill the parenting roles. In this chapter we will show you how to find and use three different sources for the parenting roles of nurturance, affirmation, and guidance. The first source is yourself, the second is another person or a support group, and the third is God.

Reparenting Yourself

Strange as it may seem, you are the person who will play the biggest role in your reparenting. When you were a child you didn't understand the painful experiences that took place in your life. You couldn't possibly parent yourself. You didn't understand that it was your parents who were unhealthy and that your pain was an outgrowth of theirs. So you locked away your vulnerable inner child, realizing that if it didn't exist, you wouldn't feel as much pain. Now, as an adult, you need to release that inner child who has been hidden away all these years and allow him or her to catch up with your growth into adulthood. You need to provide a safe place for this inner child to reveal his or her vulnerability.

Many codependent people parent themselves very harshly. They mimic the negative messages learned in childhood. If you come from a dysfunctional family, you need to recognize and get rid of the critical parent inside you. Check the messages you sometimes give yourself.

1. _____ You are stupid.
2. _____ You will never be able to do it right.
3. _____ There you go again.
4. _____ What did you expect from yourself, anyway?
5. _____ It's just not good enough.

Write at least five more critical parenting statements you tell yourself.

1. _____

2. _____

3. _____

4. _____

5. _____

Now try to remember five *positive* parenting statements from your parents or other authority figures.

1. _____

2. _____

3. _____

4. _____

5. _____

Check off the positive parenting statements you want to begin telling yourself.

1. ____That was a good try—it doesn't have to be perfect.
2. ____I'm proud of what you did today.
3. ____You are loved.
4. ____It's fun to be around you.
5. ____The world is a better place because you are in it.

Now write five more positive statements you need to tell yourself.

1. _____

2. _____

3. _____

4. _____

5. _____

Write a letter to your inner child, saying that it is safe now. Write about the pain the child felt and why it was necessary to run and hide from it. Explain that it's no longer necessary to hide, that together you can face the pain. Talk about the healing that will come as a result of coming out into the world and how essential that inner child is to your wholeness.

Dear _____,

_____

_____

_____

_____

_____

_____

_____

_____

_____

_____

_____

_____

_____

Other People

We all have people we look up to. They may not even realize how important they are to us, but we watch them, learn from them, and take special notice of the comments they make to us. These people are nurturing us, whether they know it or not! There may be some good candidates for your reparenting among the people you admire.

Write down the names of five people who have special influence on your life.

1. _____

2. _____

3. _____

4. _____

5. _____

A support group can be an excellent source for reparenting. It could be an organized group, such as Al-Anon or Adult Children of Alcoholics, or it could be an informal Bible study group.

What support groups or resources do you have in your life?

1. _____

2. _____

3. _____

Think of people who could fill the following roles in your life. Write their names after the characteristic that describes them.

1. A good listener, sounding board, and nonprofessional counselor

   _____

2. A friend with whom you share mutual support, someone who can give advice and help

   _____

3. Someone who is always there, with whom you have daily contact, even if it's very casual

4. Someone outside your family who always gives you unconditional, nonjudgmental support

_____

5. A gentle, but firm, confronter who will warn you when you're headed for trouble

_____

6. A patient helper and confidante who will work with you when you need to recycle through the ten stages to cover unfinished business and new pain

_____

7. Someone who can serve as a healthy third party in your codependent relationship with another person; someone who can take the pressure off you in a sticky situation

_____

Even if you were able to put names in each of these categories, we additionally recommend that you consider joining a support group. It's important to have outside support, especially at the beginning of the reparenting process. It's appropriate to pray for God to bring people into your life who can meet some of these needs. Don't try to hobble through reparenting on one leg. You need all three sources—yourself, others, and God—to do it successfully.

Name the "other people" you have chosen for support in the reparenting process.

1. _____

2. _____

3. _____

4. _____

5. _____

6. _____

7. _____

8. _____

THE SCREENING PROCESS

Because you are a person of worth and dignity, we want to help you make the very best choices for your "reparents." Making the wrong choices at this point can lead you back into codependent patterns. Linking up with the right people will help you achieve a strong, steady recovery. Screen your candidates for reparenting through the categories below.

A. The best "reparents" are people of the same sex. Be very cautious about choosing someone of the opposite sex. If there's even the slightest hint of a romantic entanglement, cross them off the list. When parental nurturance becomes confused with sexual fulfillment, the resulting pain and disappointment can be as devastating as incest.

B. It is wise to choose people who are in good emotional health or at an advanced stage in their own emotional recovery. At the very least, they must be further along in the recovery process than you are. Cross off anyone who is at the same stage or behind you in the recovery process.

C. It's unwise to use close family members. They're likely to bring a lot of similar unhealthy emotional baggage to the reparenting process. Cross close family members off your list.

D. Put a star beside the names of the people who have made it through your screening process. Talk to God about your list in prayer. Ask Him to make the right people available to you.

We need to make one final point about your "reparents." All people share one common trait: They are human, and they will fail. Even those people you highly respect are capable of sin and failure. You can set yourself up for hurt and disappointment if you depend too heavily on other people for your recovery. You will need to apply the principles of forgiveness, even in this reparenting stage.

I realize that my reparent may sometimes fail me.
_____ yes _____ no

I am prepared to forgive my reparent.   _____ yes _____ no

I will set healthy boundaries with my reparent so that I don't fall back into patterns of codependency.   _____ yes _____ no

God, Your Father

The highest, most consistent, and most fulfilling source for your reparenting is God. Jesus told us to call on God as "our Father in heaven." We have many promises in the Bible that God will never forsake us, even if our parents do. God offers nurturance, guidance, and protection for all his children.

God wants to adopt you into His family. When you allow Him to become your Father, you will find out—perhaps for the first time—how it feels to have a truly full love tank. God's unconditional love makes Him the best friend and counselor you can have. Your other reparents can fill your love tank to a certain point—God adds that special missing dimension. In Psalm 27:10, He promises to be with us even though our own father and mother may forsake us.

Look up each of these Bible verses. Write down what God promises to do in each of them.

In Psalm 34:18, God promises to _____

_____

In Matthew 6:8, God promises to _____

_____

In Isaiah 58:11, God promises to _____

_____

In Psalm 86:15, God promises to _____

_____

In 1 Peter 5:7, God promises to _____

_____

Children need parents who will listen carefully to their problems and give them good advice and support. God is ready to fill that role in your life.

If you could sit down face to face with God and discuss one problem, what would it be?

_____

_____

_____

Prayer is a way of talking with God. It can be silent, spoken, or written. Sharing your problems with God will help you begin to think of Him as the loving Father He is, one who is always available to you.

Write a brief note to God about the problem that is puzzling you right now.

_____

_____

_____

_____

_____

_____

_____

_____

As you go through this week, keep your spiritual ears and eyes open. God's guidance may come through thoughts you have during silent prayer, through his word, through other Christians, through sermons, or through song. There is nothing more exciting than seeing God at work in your life. Be sensitive to His guidance. Write down the ways He speaks to you.

Then you will call upon Me and go and pray to Me, and I will listen to you. And you will seek Me and find Me, when you search for Me with all your heart. I will be found by you, says the LORD. (Jer. 29:12–14)

This week I saw God working in my life in these ways:

1. _____

_____

2. _____

_____

3. _____

_____

4. _____

_____

5. _____

_____

Summary

One of the pitfalls I will have to avoid in reparenting myself is

_____

_____

Something I can do to be a good parent to myself is _____

_____

_____

Be faithful to yourself in the process of reparenting. Do a good job of setting up your supportive relationships, and you will soon reap the rewards of full recovery and good spiritual and mental health.

17. RELATIONSHIP ACCOUNTABILITY

Accountability to others is an important part of your recovery. When you make yourself accountable, you increase the probability that you will follow through on a goal. The object of this chapter is to show you how to spot trouble early on and avoid pitfalls and painful relationships.

During the past few weeks you have identified and grieved for your losses, developed a new set of perceptions, acted out new experiences based on those perceptions, and reached out to others and to God for the process of reparenting. All this renewal is wonderful. You're feeling like a new person—and rightly so! But until your new patterns become as firmly entrenched as your old patterns were, you're very vulnerable. Being open and accountable to yourself and others is an effective way to safeguard your recovery.

Relationship Inventory

What? Another inventory? Yes, but this one has a new slant. This inventory is based on current relationships, not past ones. It will reflect the way you relate to people now that your recovery is well underway.

List everyone with whom you currently have a relationship, either casual or intimate.

Work Relationships

1. _____

2. _____

3. _____

4. _____

5. _____

6. _____

Immediate Family

1. _____

2. _____

3. _____

4. _____

5. _____

6. _____

Extended Family

1. _____

2. _____

3. _____

4. _____

5. _____

6. _____

Church Relationships

1. _____

2. _____

3. _____

4. _____

5. _____

6. _____

Friends and Social Relationships

1. _____

2. _____

3. _____

4. _____

5. _____

6. _____

Other Relationships

1. _____

2. _____

3. _____

4. _____

5. _____

6. _____

Now, being very honest with yourself, go back and put a check mark beside the names of the people with whom you could easily fall back into codependent patterns.

Next, put a star beside the healthy relationships you'd like to develop further.

UNHEALTHY DEVELOPMENTS

There are six "red flags" in relationships that caution you about unhealthy developments that are brewing. Read through these categories, listing the names of people from your relationship inventory who would be likely to stray in these negative directions.

A. I will allow no physical or verbal abuse in my relationships.

Possible violators: _____

_____

B. I will allow no immoral or unethical behavior. I will not lie to cover for another person, or expect that person to stretch ethical standards to protect me. I recognize that codependents can go to unbelievable lengths (and then rationalize it in unbelievable ways) to protect persons in a close codependent relationship.

Possible violators: _____

_____

C. I will allow nothing illegal, from drug dealing and drunk driving to ignoring parking tickets. I realize that serious codependents tend to kiss off a lot of illegal activity. This must not happen in my life.

Possible violators: _____

_____

D. I will not rescue anyone. Having identified rescuing behavior as a negative part of my past relationships, I pledge not to indulge in it any more—not even "just this one little time."

Possible violators: _____

_____

E. I will not allow myself to be taken advantage of, unless I decide that God is directing me to do so. I will not be manipulated into bailing someone out (figuratively or literally). I will be sensitive to the difference between good Christian service and letting myself be a doormat or an enabler.

Possible violators: _____

_____

Accountability with Opposite-Sex Partner

HEALTHY DATING

Are you currently dating? _____ yes _____ no

This checklist will help you to be accountable to yourself for healthy dating practices.

_____ I will not date anyone who is emotionally unavailable.
_____ I will not date anyone who is morally unavailable.
_____ If any significant abuse occurs, I will consider ending the relationship immediately.

These are the qualities I would like in a dating partner.

1. _____

2. _____

3. _____

4. _____

5. _____

6. _____

I will look for these qualities before I accept a date.

_____ yes _____ no

Are you widowed or divorced?   _____ yes _____ no

The guidelines given above apply to your dating relationships as well. And there are further precautions. You will be wise to wait anywhere from three months to a year after your break-up or loss before you begin dating. Grieving people are very vulnerable to codependency. Set a timetable for dating again. It will serve as a healthy, protective boundary.

I will begin dating sometime after _____
                                           month   day   year

HEALTHY MARRIAGE

Are you married?   _____ yes _____ no

You need to be sensitive to the following issues in your marriage relationship.

A. Authority and Control

Are you maintaining a partnership in marriage?

_____ yes _____ no

Are you sharing control, with a head of the household and a responsible lieutenant?   _____ yes _____ no

How? *(For instance, my opinion and my spouse's opinion are both considered during a decision-making process.)*

_____

Are you both comfortable with the way you are sharing authority?
_____ yes _____ no

If you answered no, what are the issues you need to deal with?

1. _____

2. _____

3. _____

B. Needs and Wants

Are you meeting each other's needs comfortably?
_____ yes _____ no

What changes do you need to make in this area?

1. _____

2. _____

3. _____

C. Sexuality

Are you both free of outside sexual interests?   _____ yes _____ no

Does either of you ever use sex as a weapon to gain control?
_____ yes _____ no

Does either of you have a sexual addiction *(to pornography, flirtation, affairs)?*   _____ yes _____ no

Are you both satisfied with the degree and frequency of sexual contact?   _____ yes _____ no

If there is dissatisfaction, are you willing to sit down and talk about it?   _____ yes _____ no

When? _____

D. Emotional Support

Do you let your spouse dictate your mood?   _____ yes _____ no

Do you take the blame for your spouse's mood?
_____ yes _____ no

Are you able to continue with healthy emotions and behavior even when your spouse is in a bad mood?   _____ yes _____ no

E. Christian Service

What kinds of Christian service are you involved in?

1. _____

2. _____

3. _____

4. _____

5. _____

Do you feel you must do these things to win God's approval?
_____ yes _____ no

Do you accept some responsibilities for service just because you're afraid of saying no?   _____ yes _____ no

Do you feel you should step down from some responsibilities?
_____ yes _____ no

Check the ways you could be comfortable saying no.

_____ My schedule is just too full to take on anything else right now.

_____ I'm not available to help because I planned to spend some special time alone with my children today.

_____ Thank you for asking, but I think it's more than I can handle right now.

_____ If I take this responsibility, I will be spreading myself too thin, and my other areas of service are very important to me.

ACCOUNTABILITY

It's easy to "fudge" on promises made to yourself. But when you include another person, your promises become much more binding.

Now that I have identified the dangerous places in my

relationships, I will be accountable to *(name)* _____

_____ about them on a weekly basis. I will

record the dates of our conversations below.

Week 1 _____   Week 5 _____

Week 2 _____   Week 6 _____

Week 3 _____   Week 7 _____

Week 4 _____   Week 8 _____

Summary

How do you feel about being accountable to someone for

maintaining healthy relationships? _____

_____

_____

Are you being completely honest with that person?
_____ yes _____ no
Are you being completely honest with yourself?
_____ yes _____ no
With God?   _____ yes _____ no

18. MAINTENANCE

This is it—the last step in your climb to recovery. You can look down that long staircase behind you and remember each one of those steps. Some of them were painful. Some were sad. Some were enlightening. Others were scary and maybe a little exhilarating. Now, just as you're reaching the top, suppose life throws you a banana peel (life does that, you know). The last thing you want to do is tumble all the way back down into that dark hole of codependency. And you won't, if you're faithful to a maintenance program. Maintenance isn't superfluous—it's an integral part of your recovery. So please take it seriously.

Balancing Your Time

A healthy person keeps a balanced approach to life. Perhaps giving up your codependent behaviors has opened up some new time slots. Take a moment to consider carefully how you want to invest your time. This pie chart (p. 249) represents a typical week in your life. Draw wedges on it to show how much time you would like to spend in each of the following areas:

1. job or homemaking duties
2. family life

3. leisure and play
4. quality time with significant others
5. worship and church activities
6. time alone

7. other _____

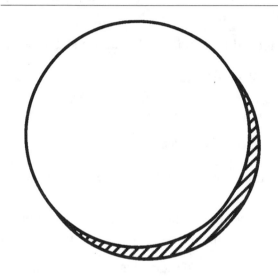

Meeting Your Needs

If you're hungry, you eat. If you itch, you scratch. If you have a need, you take care of it. That's not too complicated, right? Wrong. Look at it this way: As a codependent, you have spent years ignoring or repressing your needs, beginning with that most basic need of having your love tank filled. We've taken you through a whole process of getting in touch with your needs and finding healthy ways to meet them. Now you need to carry on that process on your own.

SPIRITUAL NEEDS

My church meets my need for worship, sound teaching, and fellowship.   _____ yes _____ no

My church provides an opportunity for meaningful service.

_____ yes _____ no

I am faithfully taking time each day to be alone with God.

_____ yes _____ no

I feel that I am growing in my personal relationship with God.

_____ yes _____ no

If you checked no for any of the above statements, what will you do

to meet that need? _____

_____

RELATIONSHIP NEEDS

Am I building a new network of support persons in my recovery journey? _____ yes _____ no

Do I have internal permission to set healthy boundaries in all of my key relationships? _____ yes _____ no

The following are four examples of how and when I have set boundaries in relationships in the past month. *(For instance, I shared with a friend that I could not continue to baby-sit for her on an "emergency basis.")*

1. _____

2. _____

3. _____

4. _____

Do I have new internal permission to be honest in expressing the full extent of my needs? _____ yes _____ no

The following are five areas of need that I have been "stuffing down." These are areas I need to express to certain key persons in my support network. *(For instance, I may need to tell my husband how much I desire to be held by him in nonsexual ways.)*

1. Key person _____

   My unexpressed need _____

   _____

2. Key person _____

   My unexpressed need _____

   _____

3. Key person _____

   My unexpressed need _____

   _____

4. Key person _____

   My unexpressed need _____

   _____

5. Key person _____

   My unexpressed need _____

   _____

WORK-RELATED NEEDS

Finish the following statements.

The thing I really like about my work is _____

_____

One stressful thing at work is _____

_____

Some things I can do to ease the stress at work are:

1. _____

2. _____

3. _____

If the stress at work becomes too great, I can _____

_____

One person who can give me good advice about handling my job

stress is _____

God's Role in Your Recovery

God is a present and powerful help in your recovery process. It's difficult to overestimate His role. God does make love a choice for you; it is no longer a compulsion. When you feel fully secure in His love, you are able to love yourself and others freely and completely.

When you accept God's friendship and help, you are actually surrendering yourself to Him. When you admit you can't master your addictions on your own, you invite God to take control. Surrender does not mean tossing the whole chunk of your life at His feet. It means consciously and willingly giving Him every part of yourself, one aspect at a time. This is the great paradox of the gospel: our loss becomes our gain. We give up our brokenness to gain wholeness.

You've written several letters as part of your recovery. This letter will be to God. In it, admit that you are powerless against your addictions. Ask for

His help, guidance, conviction, and nurturance as you continue on your journey to recovery.

Dear God,

_____

_____

_____

_____

_____

_____

_____

_____

_____

_____

_____

_____

Daily Maintenance

Your daily maintenance program will contain three elements: a devotional time, contact with the person to whom you are accountable, and a journal entry. You will need to make a regular place in your schedule for each of these elements.

DEVOTIONAL TIME

God is waiting to interact with you each day. He wants to be your loving Father, but you must give Him the time. You can draw close to God by reading His Word, the Bible, and by taking time to pray. You may wish to choose a devotional book *(Day by Day, Love Is a Choice)* or a Bible edited for recovering persons *(Serenity: A Companion for Twelve-Step Recovery)*. A Christian friend can help you get started. And remember this important fact about prayer: It's a two-way street. Don't be guilty of presenting your "shopping list" of requests to God and then tuning out. Learn to be quiet before Him. Give Him a chance to speak, to nurture you. Many people benefit from listening to God with a pencil in hand. They jot down ideas, impressions, and guidance that come to them in their quiet time. Listening to God is probably the hardest of the daily disciplines. It is also the most important.

I will have my devotional time at _____ each day.

ACCOUNTABILITY

By now you have built a support group of spiritually mature, emotionally healthy friends. These include the people you have chosen for your re-parenting process. Now you need to select one of those people to stick with you for a while. Your accountability during the maintenance stage can gradually taper off as you become secure in your new perceptions and behaviors. For the first month or so you will want to be in contact every two or three days. Then you may reduce the contact to once a week, once every two weeks, and so on. But make sure you touch on the significant issues in your life each time you talk. And if you hit some heavy weather, plan to talk daily again until the crisis is over.

I will talk to *(name)* _____ about my

progress in recovery at _____ each day.

YOUR JOURNAL

Your journal will be a kind of daily inventory of significant events and relationships. After working through this book, you're familiar with making inventories and looking them over to discover trends and patterns in your life. This is exactly what your daily journal will accomplish for you. It will keep you on top of things. If codependency problems start to rear their ugly heads, you will see red flags waving at you from the pages of your journal.

Journaling also gives you an opportunity to be faithful to yourself in reparenting. Give yourself credit when you recognize and break a bad habit, or when you develop a good, new one. Get those positive messages in writing. And keep this in mind: The key issue in living your life is not perfection, but *awareness*. Keep a finger on the pulse of your healthy and codependent behaviors. Take good care of yourself!

I will write my journal entry at _____ each day.

Keep the first week of journal entries here in the spaces below. Then purchase a notebook or diary of some kind (buy a nice one, so you'll be anxious to use it!) to continue your journaling.

Day One

Bible reading and prayer: _____

_____

_____

_____

Ways I showed negative or codependent behaviors: _____

_____

_____

Ways I showed positive or healthy behaviors: _____

_____

_____

_____

I made my accountability contact. ____ yes ___ no

General comments about the day: _____

_____

_____

Day Two

Bible reading and prayer: _____

_____

_____

Ways I showed negative or codependent behaviors: _____

_____

_____

Ways I showed positive or healthy behaviors: _____

_____

_____

_____

I made my accountability contact. ____ yes ____ no

General comments about the day: _____

_____

_____

Day Three

Bible reading and prayer: _____

_____

_____

_____

Ways I showed negative or codependent behaviors: _____

_____

_____

Ways I showed positive or healthy behaviors: _____

_____

_____

_____

I made my accountability contact.   _____ yes _____ no

General comments about the day: _____

_____

_____

Day Four

Bible reading and prayer: _____

_____

_____

_____

Ways I showed negative or codependent behaviors: _____

_____

_____

Ways I showed positive or healthy behaviors: _____

_____

_____

_____

I made my accountability contact.   _____ yes _____ no

General comments about the day: _____

_____

_____

Day Five

Bible reading and prayer: _____

_____

_____

Ways I showed negative or codependent behaviors: _____

_____

_____

Ways I showed positive or healthy behaviors: _____

_____

_____

_____

I made my accountability contact.   _____ yes _____ no

General comments about the day: _____

_____

_____

Day Six

Bible reading and prayer: _____

_____

_____

_____

Ways I showed negative or codependent behaviors: _____

_____

_____

Ways I showed positive or healthy behaviors: _____

_____

_____

_____

I made my accountability contact.   _____ yes _____ no

General comments about the day: _____

_____

_____

Day Seven

Bible reading and prayer: _____

_____

_____

_____

Ways I showed negative or codependent behaviors: _____

_____

_____

Ways I showed positive or healthy behaviors: _____

_____

_____

_____

I made my accountability contact.   _____ yes _____ no

General comments about the day: _____

_____

_____

PART
THREE

DEFINING
HEALTHY
RELATIONSHIPS

19. CODEPENDENT OR HEALTHY RELATIONSHIPS

Because codependency most often stems from problems in your family of origin, many codependents have no idea what a healthy family is or how it should work. These last two chapters are designed to fix in your mind the characteristics of healthy families and healthy relationships. You will identify your strengths as a family as well as the areas that need some continued work and growth.

We at the Minirth-Meier Clinics take great pleasure in seeing the people we counsel shed their destructive patterns and blossom into happy, fulfilled individuals. Jennifer, the perfectionistic mother, came to us depressed and driven to the point where she could go no further. After some time in counseling, Jennifer understood that she was trying to be "supermom" in order to make herself forget the pain of her past. She finally realized that love *is* a choice. She was able to choose the activities she wanted to be involved in. She also chose to open herself more completely to God and to her family. As her love tank was filled, people commented on how healthy she looked, how she smiled all the time, and how she suddenly seemed to be enjoying life. Jennifer's inner glow was real!

We sincerely hope that applying these principles has brought a similar result in your life. Now, as you work through this chapter, you will see what to keep striving for in individual and family relationships.

As you go through these exercises, you will be evaluating your *current* family, not your family of origin. If you are single and living alone, answer the questions based on your family of friends. If you are single and live with others, consider the people you live with as your family of friends.

Healthy	Codependent
We as spouses are sane and balanced. There is no depression, no mental illness, no extreme frustration with life. If depression existed in the past, it's been dealt with adequately.	One or both of us spouses are mentally unbalanced, preoccupied, frustrated, or unrealistic in our world view. If one spouse suffers from these problems, the other will be preoccupied with the problems of the mate.

Circle the statements above that describe the strengths of your current family. Underline the areas you need to target for improvement. Mark an X where you would rate your family.

Healthy   *Unhealthy*

1.......2.......3.......4.......5.......6.......7

Healthy	Codependent
Spouses are not addicted. There is no problem with compulsions, like workaholism, rageaholism, compulsive spending, or eating disorders.	Spouses are addicted to drugs, alcohol, or work. They are consumed by rage or hungers. They are driven by compulsions.

Circle the statements above that describe the strengths of your family. Underline the areas you need to target for improvement. Mark an X where you would rate your family.

Healthy   *Unhealthy*

1. . . . . . .2. . . . . . .3. . . . . . .4. . . . . . .5. . . . . . .6. 7

Healthy   Codependent

Spouses are mature,   Spouses are immature and
self-sufficient, and able to deal   tend to lean on the children
with life.   for nurturance, ego-
                                                bolstering, advice, and
                                                other kinds of help.

Circle the statements above that describe the strengths of your family. Underline the areas you need to target for improvement. Mark an X where you would rate your family.

Healthy   *Unhealthy*

1. . . . . . .2. . . . . . .3. . . . . . .4. . . . . . .5. . . . . . .6. 7

Healthy   Codependent

Spouses have a positive,   Spouses have a poorly
comfortable self-image.   developed or skewed self-
                                                image.

Circle the statements above that describe the strengths of your family. Underline the areas you need to target for improvement. Mark an X where you would rate your family.

Healthy   *Unhealthy*

1. . . . . . .2. . . . . . .3. . . . . . .4. . . . . . .5. . . . . .6. 7

Healthy

Codependent

Spouses can relate appropriately to God. In the best-case scenario, God is central to the family structure.

Spouses are in an uncomfortable relationship with God; one or both may be atheists (no relationship at all) or agnostics. Or they may be religious but intensely legalistic and rigid in their theology, insisting that the children follow in their theological footsteps.

Circle the statements above that describe the strengths of your family. Underline the areas you need to target for improvement. Mark an X where you would rate your family.

Healthy   *Unhealthy*

1. . . . . . .2. . . . . . .3. . . . . . .4. . . . . . .5. . . . . .6. 7

Healthy

Codependent

Spouses are committed to maintaining a happy marriage.

Spouses fight viciously and feel bitter toward each other and marriage in general. They may divorce or stay in a hostile relationship "for the sake of the kids."

Circle the statements above that describe the strengths of your family. Underline the areas you need to target for improvement. Mark an X where you would rate your family.

Healthy   *Unhealthy*

1. . . . . . .2. . . . . .3. . . . . .4. . . . . .5. . . . . .6. 7

Codependency Check-up

1. Codependents suffer from an unclear or faulty self-image and therefore tend to become absorbed into other people.

Check the words that describe you:

_____ strong   _____ overly dependent on others
_____ lacking confidence   _____ self-sufficient
_____ content   _____ feeling good about myself
_____ down on myself   _____ out of control
_____ a person of worth   _____ worthless and unloved

Rate your self-image on a scale of one to ten, one being low, and ten high.

1   2   3   4   5   6   7   8   9   10

2. Codependents become confusingly enmeshed with others and entangle their identity with those they love.

I have healthy boundaries with:

_____ my spouse   _____ my colleagues
_____ my children   _____ my church friends
_____ my in-laws   _____ my parents
_____ my friends in general

Put an X beside the relationships that still lack healthy boundaries.

Review the section on establishing boundaries in chapter 15.

How will you work to establish healthy boundaries in the

relationships in which they are lacking? _____

_____

_____

3. Because codependents' love tanks have been running on empty, they cannot understand and recognize unconditional love. Codependents will confuse love with infatuation, mutual love hunger, physical attraction, and simple affection.

I now understand that true love is _____

_____

_____

_____

4. Codependents bring addictions and compulsiveness to their personal relationships. It's easy for them to become obsessed with controlling others.

_____ I don't have to be obsessed with controlling other people because the only person I can really control is myself.

_____ I still see a tendency to want to control

(*name*) _____

CODEPENDENCY AND MARRIAGE

It's good for couples to reexamine their marriage expectations periodically. Even healthy couples tend to have some codependent reasons for having chosen each other. People, circumstances, feelings, and needs all change. Marriage partners need to respond appropriately.

The codependent reasons I married my spouse are:

_____ to rescue or take care of him/her.
_____ to have someone take care of me.
_____ to have someone to replace my parents.
_____ to try to resolve the pain from my family or origin.

The new reasons I am choosing to be married to my spouse today are:

_____ I have a strong, permanent commitment to my spouse.
_____ My marriage brings emotional, physical, and financial security to me, my spouse, and my children.
_____ I love my spouse.
_____ I want to obey God's laws about marriage.
_____ I'm coming to the marriage as a whole person with important things to give and receive.

CODEPENDENCY AND FAMILY RELATIONSHIPS

Look over this list of characteristics of a healthy family. Check the ones that describe your family. Put a star beside the ones you need to work on and write a brief note about how you will begin to work on them. (Remember, you can take responsibility only for your own behavior. Others may or may not be willing to change.)

1. _____ We have fun and laugh together.
2. _____ We encourage and compliment one another.
3. _____ We respect each other's privacy.
4. _____ We cooperate with each other.
5. _____ We express anger appropriately.
6. _____ We are willing to negotiate and compromise.
7. _____ We unconditionally love each other.

8. ____ We talk about our feelings.

9. ____ We work through conflicts.

10. ____ We can be silly sometimes.

11. ____ We are not afraid to admit failure.

12. ____ Everyone is willing to say "I was wrong" when it's appropriate.

13. ____ Everyone is treated equally.

14. ____ We allow each other to make mistakes.

15. ____ We share what we have with each other.

16. ____ Our individuality is encouraged.

Summary

How many healthy family characteristics did you mark? _____
What does this tell you about the health of your family?
*(For instance, we've come a long way, but we still have
some things to work on.)*

_____

_____

_____

Choose one healthy family characteristic you'd like to work on and
write it here.

_____

_____

How will you share this goal with your family?

_____

_____

What will you do if you share your hopes, but your family doesn't want to change? *(For instance, I will go ahead and model the behavior myself, and I will deal with my feelings of hurt and anger.)*

_____

_____

_____

Remember, there are resources beyond your family for meeting your needs. If your spouse or other members of your family are unwilling to participate in the recovery process, don't despair. A close relationship with God will help you continue to love and forgive them. And the emotional support you get from your church, your support group, your counselor, or your network of healthy friends will keep you on track in your own recovery.

20. Making Relationships Work

The very best relationships have their ups and downs. Stress factors that we have absolutely no control over—loss of a job, major illness, a death in the family—can put quite a strain on even the healthiest relationships. When that happens, it's easy to fall back into codependent patterns.

Think of this chapter as a kind of insurance policy against codependency. If, at some point in the future, you find yourself slipping into codependent patterns, come back to this chapter and work through the steps of fine-tuning your relationships.

Balancing Dependence and Independence

The opposite of codependency is not independence. It is interdependence. Imagine a relationship wheel that looks like a clock with the hands pointing to twelve. This represents a healthy, interdependent relationship. As we travel the circle in a clockwise direction, we tip the scale toward independence. The further we go, the more deeply we get into independent attitudes. The partners develop separate interests, priorities, and schedules until at some point they realize that they have become strangers.

Counterclockwise motion indicates an exaggerated dependence in the relationship. In this situation, one or both partners may begin to lean excessively on the other. Healthy boundaries gradually disappear, and the old co-dependent need to control takes over once more.

In a healthy relationship, the individuals will work back up toward the top of the circle. The first step in reestablishing the right balance is to decide which way the wheel has swung.

ANALYZING MY RELATIONSHIP WITH *(name)* _____

1. _____ I hardly know this person anymore.
2. _____ It's so hard on me when we have to be apart.
3. _____ I've been depending on this person to meet nearly all my needs.
4. _____ I feel uncomfortable if I don't know exactly where this person is and what he/she is doing.
5. _____ I miss the togetherness we once shared.
6. _____ I'm afraid to tell him/her what my needs are.

Numbers 1, 5, and 6 indicate a relationship that has swung toward exaggerated independence. Numbers 2, 3, and 4 indicate a relationship that is moving toward excessive dependency.

If you have swung toward exaggerated independence in a relationship, you will want to consider the four steps to correcting an overly independent relationship. If you have become excessively dependent in a relationship, you will want to consider the six steps to correcting an excessively dependent relationship.

Under each step write ways you might apply that particular step to your relationship.

CORRECTING AN OVERLY INDEPENDENT RELATIONSHIP

Step 1

Admit that a problem exists and that it's time to do something about it. *(For instance, I admit that you and I have become strangers, and I don't know how to restore our intimacy.)*

_____

_____

Step 2

Do a time inventory to discover what is stealing the time you once shared. *(For instance, my time inventory reveals that far too much of my time and energy is being poured into my workaholism.)*

_____

_____

Step 3

Make new priorities with a commitment to remove the things that are standing in the way of your relationship. *(For instance, I pledge to limit my vocational work week to a maximum of 45 hours.)*

_____

_____

Step 4

Decide on a way to be accountable for maintaining the commitments made in Step 3. *(For instance, I shall begin attending meetings of Workaholics Anonymous and ask my program sponsor to confront me if I begin to violate these boundaries.)*

_____

_____

CORRECTING AN EXCESSIVELY DEPENDENT RELATIONSHIP

Step 1

Acknowledge the problem. *(For instance, I expect you, my spouse, to always be my therapist.)*

Step 2

Take an inventory of which boundaries are being violated. *(For instance, I expect you to be emotionally available to hear my pain twenty-four hours a day.)*

Step 3

Both people declare the boundaries they believe are appropriate. *(For instance, my spouse will tell me if his own emotional pain or fatigue is of such magnitude that he cannot respond to my pain at the moment.)*

Step 4

Both people make up a list of what they are willing to give up. *(For instance, I surrender the magical expectation that you will always be able to remove my pain for me.)*

Step 5

Each person makes a commitment to care of himself/herself and to take responsibility for himself/herself. *(For instance, I am committing to attend at least two meetings of Codependents Anonymous per week as a means of releasing some of my pain outside of our relationship.)*

_____

_____

Step 6

To help maintain the relationship, both the leaning and the codependent partner develop healthy outside interests. *(For instance, I plan to fulfill my longtime dream of completing my college education by enrolling in evening courses.)*

_____

_____

These guidelines will work in helping you to correct a broad spectrum of relationships, including those at work, with close friends, with family members, and in your marriage. Learning to spot and deal with trouble early on is a benefit that we hope you'll carry from this study through the rest of your life.

Summary

At the Minirth-Meier Clinics when we're about to bring the counseling process to a close, we like to have people review their progress.

In what ways have you changed as you've worked through this book?

1. _____

2. _____

3. _____

4. _____

5. _____

6. _____

7. _____

8. _____

9. _____

10. _____

List the relationships that have become more healthy as you've worked through the recovery process.

1. _____

2. _____

3. _____

4. _____

5. _____

6. _____

7. _____

8. _____

9. _____

10. _____

What accomplishments are you most proud of?

1. _____

2. _____

3. _____

4. _____

5. _____

6. _____

7. _____

8. _____

9. _____

10. _____

Don't be surprised if at some point you find yourself needing to cycle back through the ten stages of recovery. We have given you some tools to understand and change your unhealthy codependent behavior. But codependency won't magically go away. You need to apply these principles for healthy relationships throughout your lifetime. If you get stuck or need help in the process, please don't hesitate to seek out the help you need.

As you look back through this book, you will see the progress you have made. We are proud of you for being open to new discoveries and new experiences. You should be proud of yourself, too. Celebrate your recovery and keep pressing on for healthy relationships that honor God.

About the Authors

Robert Hemfelt, Ed.D., is a psychologist who specializes in the treatment of chemical dependencies, codependency, and compulsivity disorders. Before joining the Minirth-Meier Clinics, he was formerly the supervisor of therapeutic services for the Substance Abuse Study Clinic of the Texas Research Institute of Mental Sciences. He has co-authored numerous books, including *We Are Driven, Love Is a Choice,* and *Love Hunger.*

Frank Minirth, M.D., is a diplomate of the American Board of Psychiatry and Neurology and received his M.D. degree from the University of Arkansas College of Medicine.

Paul Meier, M.D., received an M.S. degree in cardiovascular physiology at Michigan State University and an M.D. degree from the University of Arkansas College of Medicine. He completed his psychiatric residency at Duke University.

Dr. Minirth and Dr. Meier founded the Minirth-Meier Clinic in Richardson, Texas, one of the largest psychiatric clinics in the world, with associated clinics in Chicago; Newport Beach, Palm Springs, Los Angeles, Orange, San Diego, and Laguna Hills, California; Little Rock, Arkansas; Longview, Fort Worth, Sherman, San Antonio, and Austin, Texas; and Washington, D.C. Both Dr. Minirth and Dr. Meier received degrees from Dallas Theological

Seminary. They have also co-authored more than thirty books, including *Love Hunger, Love Is a Choice, Happiness Is a Choice, Worry-Free Living, Free to Forgive, A Walk with the Serenity Prayer,* and *We Are Driven*.

Deborah Newman is a psychotherapist with the Minirth-Meier Clinics. She was graduated from Oxford Graduate School, Grace Theological Seminary, and Bryan College.

Brian Newman is the Clinical Director of Inpatient Services at the Minirth-Meier Clinic in Richardson, Texas. He was graduated from Oxford Graduate School, Grace Theological Seminary, and the University of Alabama.